Ephes

God's Master Plan

JOHN A. STEWART

Lamplighters International is a Christian ministry that helps individuals engage with God and His Word and equips believers to be disciple-makers.

For additional information about Lamplighters ministry resources, contact:

Lamplighters International
771 NE Harding Street, Suite 250
Minneapolis, MN USA 55413
or visit our website at
www.LamplightersUSA.org.

Product Code Ep-NK-2P

ISBN 978-1-931372-64-0

Contents

How to Use This Study

What Is Lamplighters?

Lamplighters is a Christian ministry that helps individuals engage with God and His Word and equips believers to be disciple-makers. This Bible study, comprising ten individual lessons, is a self-contained unit and an integral part of the entire discipleship ministry. When you have completed the study, you will have a much greater understanding of a portion of God's Word, with many new truths that you can apply to your life.

How to study a Lamplighters Lesson

A Lamplighters study begins with prayer, your Bible, the weekly lesson, and a sincere desire to learn more about God's Word. The questions are presented in a progressive sequence as you work through the study material. You should not use Bible commentaries or other reference books (except a dictionary) until you have completed your weekly lesson and met with your weekly group. Approaching the Bible study in this way allows you to personally encounter many valuable spiritual truths from the Word of God.

To gain the most out of the Bible study, find a quiet place to complete your weekly lesson. Each lesson will take approximately 45–60 minutes to complete. You will likely spend more time on the first few lessons until you are familiar with the format, and our prayer is that each week will bring the discovery of important life principles.

The writing space within the weekly studies provides the opportunity for you to answer questions and respond to what you have learned. Putting answers in your own words, and including Scripture references where appropriate, will help you personalize and commit to memory the truths you have learned. The answers to the questions will be found in the Scripture references at the end of each question or in the passages listed at the beginning of each lesson.

If you are part of a small group, it's a good idea to record the specific dates that you'll be meeting to do the individual lessons. Record the specific dates each time the group will be meeting next to the lesson titles on the Contents page. Additional lines have been provided for you to record when you go through this same study at a later date.

The side margins in the lessons can be used for the spiritual insights you glean from other group or class members. Recording these spiritual truths will likely be a spiritual help to you and others when you go through this study again in the future.

Audio Introduction

A brief audio introduction is available to help you learn about the historical background of the book, gain an understanding of its theme and structure, and be introduced to some of the major truths. Audio introductions are available for all Lamplighters studies and are a great resource for the group leader; they can also be used to introduce the study to your group. To access the audio introductions, go to www.LamplightersUSA.org.

"*Do You Think?*" Questions

Each weekly study has a few *"do you think?"* questions designed to help you to make personal applications from the biblical truths you are learning. In the first lesson the *"do you think?"* questions are placed in italic print for easy identification. If you are part of a study group, your insightful answers to these questions could be a great source of spiritual encouragement to others.

Personal Questions

Occasionally you'll be asked to respond to personal questions. If you are part of a study group you may choose not to share your answers to these questions with the others. However, be sure to answer them for your own benefit because they will help you compare your present level of spiritual maturity to the biblical principles presented in the lesson.

A Final Word

Throughout this study the masculine pronouns are frequently used in the generic sense to avoid awkward sentence construction. When the pronouns *he*, *him*, and *his* are used in reference to the Trinity (God the Father, Jesus Christ, and the Holy Spirit), they always refer to the masculine gender.

This Lamplighters study was written after many hours of careful preparation. It is our prayer that it will help you "... grow in the grace and knowledge of our Lord and Savior Jesus Christ. To Him be the glory both now and forever. Amen" (2 Peter 3:18).

What Is an Intentional Discipleship Bible Study?

The *Next Step* in Bible Study

The Lamplighters Bible study series is ideal for individual, small group, and classroom use. This Bible study is also designed for Intentional Discipleship training. An Intentional Discipleship (ID) Bible study has four key components. Individually they are not unique, but together they form the powerful core of the ID Bible study process.

1. Objective: Lamplighters is a discipleship training ministry that has a dual objective: (1) to help individuals engage with God and His Word and (2) to equip believers to be disciple-makers. The small group format provides extensive opportunity for ministry training, and it's not limited by facilities, finances, or a lack of leadership staffing.

2. Content: The Bible is the focus rather than Christian books. Answers to the study questions are included within the study guides, so the theology is in the study material, not in the leader's mind. This accomplishes two key objectives: (1) It gives the group leader confidence to lead another individual or small group without fear, and (2) it protects the small group from theological error.

3. Process: The ID Bible study process begins with an Open House, which is followed by a 6–14-week study, which is followed by a presentation of the Final Exam (see graphic on page 8). This process provides a natural environment for continuous spiritual growth and leadership development.

4. Leadership Development: As group participants grow in Christ, they naturally invite others to the groups. The leader-trainer (1) identifies and recruits new potential leaders from within the group, (2) helps them register for online discipleship training, and (3) provides in-class leadership mentoring until they are both competent and confident to lead a group according to the ID Bible study process. This leadership development process is scalable, progressive, and comprehensive.

Overview of the Leadership Training and Development Process

*

There are three stages of leadership training in the Intentional Discipleship process: (1) leading studies, (2) training leaders, and (3) multiplying groups (see appendix for greater detail).

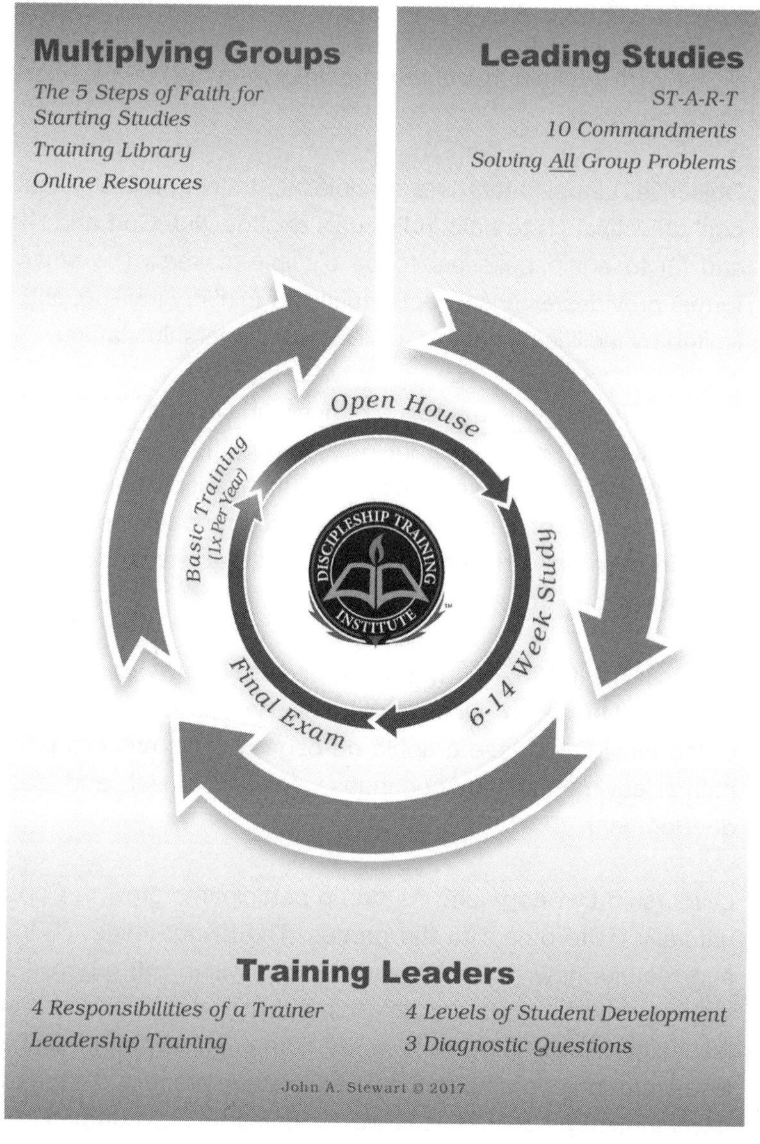

How Can I Be Trained?

Included within this Bible study is the student workbook for Level 1 (Basic Training). Level 1 training is both free and optional. Level 1 training teaches you a simple 4-step process (ST-A-R-T) to help you prepare a life-changing Bible study and 10 proven small group leadership principles that will help your group thrive. To register for a Level 1 online training event, either as an individual or as a small group, go to www.LamplightersUSA.org/training or www.discipleUSA.org. If you have additional questions, you can also call 800-507-9516.

www.LamplightersUSA.org/training
or
www.discipleUSA.org

Introduction

"What in the world is God doing?" "Is this life just one big experiment—a giant test conducted by God—and we were never given the pre-test instructions?" Sometimes it feels that way.

Ephesians is God's master guide plan and His divine blueprint for this world and all creation. But not only does Ephesians reveal God's master plan; it also answers another great question about life "Why am I here?" God's answers to these two great questions will thrill your heart and transform your life.

Historical Background

Ephesians was written by the apostle Paul (Ephesians 1:1) under the inspiration of the Holy Spirit while he was in prison (Ephesians 4:1). The letter was likely delivered by Tychicus, who also informed the Ephesian believers of Paul's well-being (Ephesians 6:21).

Paul first visited Ephesus during his second missionary journey (Acts 18:19–21). The city of Ephesus, located in what is now western Turkey, was a leading commercial and cultural center in the Roman Empire. On Paul's third missionary journey he spent three years at Ephesus where he preached the gospel and ministered at the school of Tyrannus (Acts 19:10). Everyone in the Roman province of Asia heard the word of the Lord during this time (Acts 19:10).

Paul's message of salvation in Christ alone through faith alone angered the local merchants who sold idols and silver shrines. This led to a riot and Paul was forced to leave the city (Acts 19:17–20:1). At the end of Paul's third missionary journey on his return to Jerusalem, he met briefly with the Ephesian elders at Miletus to encourage them to remain faithful to the Lord and to avoid false teachers (Acts 20:13–35).

Theme

The book of Ephesians reveals God's master plan (Ephesians 1:9–11; 3:8–11). The Bible says, **having made known to us the mystery of His will, according to His good pleasure which He purposed in Himself, that in the dispensation of the fullness of the times He might gather together in one all things in Christ, both which are in heaven and on earth—in Him** (Ephesians 1:9–10). Or to put it in simpler terms: "God is bringing everything on earth and in heaven together under the sovereign authority of Jesus Christ according to His perfect timing." In the New Living Translation (NLT), verse 10 reads, "And this is his [God's] plan: At the right time God will bring everything together under the authority of Christ—everything in heaven and on earth."

What will this look like? The book of Philippians gives us a glimpse. The Bible says, **that at the name of Jesus every knee should bow, of those in heaven, and of those on earth, and those under the earth, and that every tongue should confess that Jesus Christ is Lord, to the glory of God the Father** (Philippians 2:10–11). This doesn't mean everyone will be saved. It means that everyone who has ever lived—small and great, rich and poor—will acknowledge that Jesus Christ is God to the glory of God, the Father. The unsaved will confess Jesus Christ is Lord in everlasting judgment; the saved will confess Jesus Christ as Lord in everlasting praise and exultation.

Five Unique Characteristics

A letter or a treatise? Unlike many of Paul's letters to the churches, there is no particular problem addressed in Ephesians and no personal greetings are extended to friends or co-laborers. Ephesians reads more like a doctrinal treatise on God's grand purpose and plan than it does a personal letter to a church or group of churches.

The heavenlies. Paul's letter begins with the statement that God has blessed believers with every spiritual blessing in the heavenlies (Ephesians 1:3 KJV). Different Bible versions translate the Greek word (*epouranios*) as "heavenly realms" (NIV) and "heavenly places" (NKJV, NASB). The word refers to the unseen, spiritual dimension of life where Christ rules supremely and the realm in which believers can experience the manifold fruit of their relationship with Christ through the power of the Holy Spirit.

Mystery. The Greek word for *mystery* means "a truth that was formerly hidden by God but has now been revealed." This word is used six times in Ephesians (vs. 1:9; 3:3–4, 9; 5:32; 6:19) and is used frequently in Paul's other writings—all with the same meaning.

Riches. Paul's use of the word *riches* is another of his frequent metaphors. The phrases **riches of His grace** (Ephesians 1:7; 2:7), **the riches of His glory** (Ephesians 1:18; 3:16) and **the unsearchable riches of Christ** (Ephesians 3:8) refer to the different aspects of the incalculable inheritance that all believers are given because of their relationship to Jesus Christ.

Spiritual conflict: Ephesians, more than any other book in the Bible, reveals the nature of the intense spiritual conflict that every believer faces in this world and what the believer must do to overcome evil.

Spiritual Value

Ephesians is a truly amazing book. The book reveals God's grand eternal purpose and plan and explains how you can join Him as He accomplishes His sovereign will. Ephesians takes you into the heavenlies and reveals God's great inheritance for all believers—the riches of Christ. In doing so, the book reveals why a Christian should view life from a "heaven-to-earth" perspective rather than an "earth-to-heaven" perspective. But Ephesians doesn't chasten you with guilt-ridden invectives to get you to pursue Christ. It calls you to something much, much better—something more transcendent than what life on earth offers.

Studying Ephesians will leave you longing for more of Christ. Ephesians teaches you that whatever you think about God, He's more and He has more grace, more blessing, and more power for you to live righteously than you ever imagined. Ephesians removes all doubt about what it means to live for Jesus Christ. The question "Why am I here?" is answered conclusively in chapters 4–6 where Paul presents the "five walks" of the believer—each one detailing a key aspect of becoming an imitator of God.

Paul's letter to the Ephesians will give you a greater thirst for God. It will teach you how to access the riches of Christ and how to walk with Him. When you humble yourself and study Ephesians thoroughly, God will take you into the heavenlies and bring you back a changed person. Now may you fully realize the great inheritance God has given you in Christ, and may you surrender your entire life to Him and live "in the heavenlies" through faith.

ONE

GOD'S MASTER PLAN

Read Introduction, Ephesians 1:1–14; other references as given.

Imagine sitting in an estate attorney's office waiting to hear the reading of your grandfather's will. Many times he told you with a smile that someday he was going to make you very wealthy. Now, grieved by his passing, your mind wanders as you reflect upon his comment. When the attorney reads your grandfather's will, you are overwhelmed by his generosity and amazed by your newfound fortune. Your life will never be the same.

Ephesians 1:3–14 reveals a first look at God's master plan and lists four spiritual aspects of a Christian's divine inheritance (adoption, acceptance, redemption, sealing). Reading about your spiritual inheritance will thrill your heart; understanding your spiritual inheritance will change your life.

Now before you begin this and every lesson, ask God to reveal Jesus Christ to you and to transform you into His image.

1. a. What is the central theme of Ephesians (see Introduction)?

   ...to bring everything together under the sovereign authority of Christ - everything in heaven + on earth.

   b. What two important questions does Ephesians answer (see Introduction)?

   1. What in the world is God doing?
   2. Why am I here?

Lombardi Time Rule:

If the leader arrives early, he or she has time to pray, prepare the room, and greet others personally.

ADD GROUP INSIGHTS BELOW

ADDITIONAL INSIGHTS

2. Paul identifies himself as an apostle (Greek *apostolos*—one sent or commissioned by another; in this case, God). The letter is addressed **to the saints who are in Ephesus** (Ephesians 1:1). To whom was Paul referring when he used the word **saints** (Ephesians 1:15; Romans 12:13; 1 Corinthians 1:2; Ephesians 4:12)?

   Believers - All N. T. believers; All who have placed their faith in Christ; see I Cor. 1:2; 3:1-4

3. Paul identifies his audience and offers a familiar New Testament greeting (**grace to you and peace,** Ephesians 1:1–2). Some people search for peace in personal and professional success, interpersonal relationships, and individual achievement. Others give up their search for this elusive treasure and turn to entertainment or resort to self-medication, including the use of prescription and non-prescription drugs.

   a. Peace is one of man's greatest desires, but relatively few can even define it. What is peace? Faith in God & His will -

   b. Where have you found lasting peace in your life?

      Only when I feel God's Presence & hear His voice -

   c. *Do you think* an individual can truly experience peace without knowing God's grace (salvation)? Why?

      No - Because we are too enveloped in the things of the world - Too conditioned to solve our own problems -
      Job. 13:15 ; Acts 16: 20-25 ; Phil 1: 19-26

4. In Ephesians 1:3 Paul praises God for the spiritual blessings He bestows on those chosen for salvation (Ephesians 1:3–13). In the Greek New Testament, Ephesians 1:3–14 forms one long sentence, likely emphasizing the fact that these spiritual blessings are the rightful inheritance of every believer. What and where are the **heavenly *places*** (*places* [NIV: "realms"] is italicized to indicate it was added by the translators) where believers have been blessed (Ephesians 1:3, 20; 2:6; 3:10; 6:12)? Answer in your own words.

The Third Heaven —
where Christ is now —

5. a. The term **heavenlies** (heavenly places) refers to a place or realm to which many Christians only give a passing thought. Yet it's the place or realm where God has blessed all believers with His great spiritual blessings (Ephesians 1:3). What *do you think* are these blessings that every believer possesses?

union with Christ; seated with Him in heaven; adoption; redemption; election; service abilities ... at the time of salvation —

b. Since the **heavenlies** (heavenly places) are the repository or storeroom of God's great blessings, what can a Christian do to access them in increased measure (2 Corinthians 4:18; John 6:29; Hebrews 11:1)?

Believe in Christ - Repent

6. Beginning in Ephesians 1:4 the Bible begins to reveal the first aspect of God's master plan—man's redemption.

Zip-It Rule:

Group members should agree to disagree, but should never be disagreable.

ADDITIONAL INSIGHTS

ADDITIONAL INSIGHTS

God's plan for man's redemption was devised before the foundation of the world (Ephesians 1:4), was done by a volitional choice on His part (Ephesians 1:4), and was done according to the good pleasure of His will (Ephesians 1:5). If you are saved (born again), it's not because you chose Christ; it's because He chose you (Ephesians 1:4). For what purpose (the question "Why am I here?) did God choose those who are saved (Ephesians 1:4, 6, 12)?

1. To be Holy + Blameless in His sight (v. 4)

2. to the praise of His glorious Grace v6 so that we... might bring (v. 12) Praise to His glory for all He did for us

7. God's motive for extending salvation to man is love, and man's redemption was accomplished according to the good pleasure of His will (Ephesians 1:4–5). The phrases **He chose us ... before the foundation of the world** and **having predestined us** (Ephesians 1:4–5) imply that God choses only specific people for salvation, and by consequence, the rest are not chosen and eternally lost. Other passages in the Bible appear to teach that anyone who truly repents and believes in Christ alone for eternal life can be saved (John 3:16; Acts 17:30; Romans 10:13; 1 John 2:2; 4:10). Do you believe that only certain people (those whom God predestined) can be saved, or do you believe anyone can be saved if he or she trusts in Jesus Christ completely for salvation? Why?

I believe Anyone can be saved - But because we have free will some choose not to follow the way. These people need lots of intercessory prayer to help them -

8. A person is adopted into God's family when he or she is saved (born again, redeemed). When Paul used the word **adoption** (Gk. *niothesia*), he borrowed a common image from Roman culture. A father chose to formally adopt his own son at a particular age. The adoption was done solely at the discretion of the father, was irreversible, and included an irrevocable inheritance. List three ways *you think* Paul's comparison of the Roman concept of adoption to redemption presents an accurate picture of salvation.

   1. Because it is the Father's decision - nothing to do with son

   2. Irreversible

   3. Irrevocable inheritance to the child = inheritance believers receive in Christ

9. Another aspect of a believer's spiritual inheritance in Christ is redemption (Ephesians 1:7). The word **redemption** (Gk. *apolutrosis*—purchasing with a price) refers to the price Jesus Christ paid for man's salvation. List four things the Bible says about this redemption (Ephesians 1:7).

   1. There is salvation in no other one than Christ

   2. Forgiveness of our Trespasses

   3. Is settled & secure —

   4. Christian is saved "through His blood

10. In Ephesians 1:10 the Bible gives us the first official statement of God's master plan. Even though God's plan includes

Want to learn how to disciple another person, lead a life-changing Bible study or start another study? Go to www.LamplightersUSA.org/training to learn how.

ADDITIONAL INSIGHTS

ADDITIONAL INSIGHTS

man's salvation, it extends far beyond his redemption. In your own words restate God's master plan, trying to capture the full extent of His plan with your answer (Ephesians 1:10; 3:8–11; Romans 8:18–23).

____

____

____

____

11. The first aspect of God's master plan—man's redemption through faith in Christ alone—was determined before the foundation of the world (Ephesians 1:4), involved a choice on His part (Ephesians 1:4), and was done in love (Ephesians 1:4) according to the kind intention of His will (Ephesians 1:5, 9). What must happen before this eternal transaction is completed in the life of an individual, and what do all new believers receive as God's pledge of their redemption (Ephesians 1:13–14)?

____

____

____

____

12. Now that you see that God's plan of redemption was accomplished entirely by Christ's sacrifice on your behalf, are you absolutely sure that you are saved?

    Yes / No / I'm not sure

    If you are not sure, turn to the back of this Bible study guide and read the Final Exam. It will explain how to be born again according to the Bible.

Two

Claiming Your Inheritance

Read Ephesians 1:15–23; other references as given.

In the first lesson the question asked was "What in the world is God doing?" God is gathering **together in one all things in Christ, both which are in heaven and which are on earth—in Him** (Ephesians 1:10). God is bringing about a restoration of all things—things in heaven and on earth—according to His divine will and plan.

The second question ("Why am I here?") was also answered. If you are a Christian, you have been redeemed to live to the praise of God's glory and to live a holy and blameless life (Ephesians 1:4, 12). But not all Christians know God's plan or why they are here on earth. Many believers, ignorant of God's master plan and their place within His will, pursue their own goals and forfeit the peace and blessings He has promised them.

In Ephesians 1:15–23 Paul offers a passionate prayer on behalf of the Ephesians (and all believers) to help them comprehend God's master plan and experience their full inheritance in Christ. In this passage you'll learn that there is more to salvation than merely trusting Jesus Christ and knowing where you'll spend eternity.

Before you begin, ask God to reveal Jesus Christ to you and to transform you into His image.

1. God's plan to restore all things under the supreme authority of Jesus Christ begins with the salvation of man. Each member of the Godhead or Trinity (Father, Son, and Holy

Volunteer Rule:

If the leader asks for volunteers to read, pray, and answer the questions, group members will be more inclined to invite newcomers.

ADD GROUP INSIGHTS BELOW

ADDITIONAL INSIGHTS

Spirit) is actively involved in the believer's redemption. It was the Father's plan (Ephesians 1:4; John 3:16; Acts 2:22–23), the Son's sacrifice (Ephesians 1:7; Romans 5:8), and the Holy Spirit's sealing that work together to secure man's redemption (Ephesians 1:13–14; Titus 3:5).

a. In Ephesians 1:15 the words **Therefore I also** (NIV: "For this reason") indicate a change of subject from theological truth to practical application. What was Paul's response to the great theological truths (Ephesians 1:3–14) he wrote about under the inspiration of the Holy Spirit (Ephesians 1:15–16)?

____

____

____

b. Biblical truth should always lead believers to practical application and life change. How has your life changed since you first learned about God's master plan and your great spiritual inheritance (adoption, acceptance, redemption, forgiveness, inheritance, and the sealing of the Holy Spirit)?

____

____

____

____

2. What two things did the writer of Hebrews say to his readers about the relationship between truth and personal application (Hebrews 4:1–2)?

1. ______________________________

______________________________ (v. _____)

2. ______________________________

______________________________ (v. _____)

3. In Ephesians 1:15 Paul commends his readers for their faith in Jesus Christ and their love for all the saints. Since Paul could not be with them personally, he did three things to bless them: (1) he commended them, (2) he prayed for them, and (3) he told them that he was praying for them. But rather than offering a general prayer ("God bless all the people of the world all the time"), Paul prayed specifically and intentionally for their spiritual advancement.

   a. What did Paul pray on behalf of the Ephesian believers (Ephesians 1:17)?

   ____

   ____

   b. What did Paul ask God to give them specifically (Ephesians 1:18a [first portion of the verse])?

   ____

   ____

   c. When you pray for others, in what ways do you pray *specifically* for their spiritual growth?

   ____

   ____

   ____

4. Spiritual blindness can be defined as the inability to understand and comprehend biblical truth. The reality of spiritual blindness and the need to overcome it through the power of God is a common theme throughout Scripture. List three things the Bible teaches about the spiritual blindness of the unsaved.

   John 3:19–20: ______________________________

   ____

   1 Corinthians 2:14: ______________________________

59:59 Rule:

Participants appreciate when the leader starts and finishes the studies on time—all in one hour (the 59:59 rule). If the leader doesn't complete the entire lesson, the participants will be less likely to do their weekly lessons and the Bible study discussion will tend to wander.

ADDITIONAL INSIGHTS

ADDITIONAL INSIGHTS

____

2 Corinthians 4:3–4: ______________________________

____

5. Spiritual blindness is not a characteristic exclusively of the unsaved. List four reasons all people, including believers, experience spiritual blindness.

   Mark 4:13–15 ______________________________

   ____

   Mark 4:16–17: ______________________________

   ____

   Mark 4:18–19: ______________________________

   ____

   Hebrews 5:12–14: ______________________________

   ____

6. Paul asked God to give the Ephesians **the spirit of wisdom and revelation in the knowledge of Him** [God] (Ephesians 1:17) and for **the eyes of** [their] **understanding** [to be] **enlightened** (Ephesians 1:18). What exactly was Paul asking God to do for the Ephesian believers?

   ____

   ____

   ____

7. List three things Paul asked God for on behalf of the Ephesian Christians (Ephesians 1:18–19).

   1. ______________________________

      ______________________________ (v. _____)

   2. ______________________________

      ______________________________ (v. _____)

3. ____

______________________________________ (v. ____)

8. a. In the phrase **the hope of His calling** (Ephesians 1:18), the Greek word (*elpis*) for "hope" means an absolute assurance of a future event. In the English language, hope generally refers to a wishful expectation (*I hope it doesn't rain today*). Now that you know the Greek meaning for **hope,** restate what Paul is asking God to reveal to the Ephesian believers?

____

____

____

b. Do you have this same hope (complete assurance of your eternal relationship with God)? Yes / No

Why? ____

____

____

9. Paul also asked God to reveal the **riches of the glory of His** [God's] **inheritance in the saints** (Ephesians 1:18). Just as God gives believers an inheritance (**the riches of His grace in His kindness toward us in Christ Jesus**; Ephesians 2:7), Christians are God's inheritance. God also wants believers to know that the power He used to raise Jesus Christ from the grave is available to them. What were the results of the power that raised Jesus from the dead? In other words, to what extent was Jesus raised (Ephesians 1:20–23)?

____

____

____

____

____

35% Rule:

If the leader talks more than 35% of the time, the group members will be less likely to participate.

ADDITIONAL INSIGHTS

ADDITIONAL INSIGHTS

10. List four life-changing benefits of this resurrection power that is available to all Christians.

    1. 1 Corinthians 10:13: ______________________________

    ____

    ____

    2. 1 Corinthians 15:55–57: ___________________________

    ____

    ____

    3. Ephesians 2:6: _________________________________

    ____

    ____

    4. Colossians 1:13: _______________________________

    ____

    ____

THREE

HEART OF THE PROBLEM

Read Ephesians 2:1–10; other references as given.

In the previous lesson Paul prayed the Ephesian believers would believe. He prayed they would *believe* God really saved them (**the hope** [complete assurance] **of His calling**, Ephesians 1:18). He prayed they would *believe* they were God's chosen inheritance (Ephesians 1:18). Lastly, he prayed they would *believe* the power that resurrected Jesus Christ from the grave was within them.

But why does man need to be saved? What's wrong with him? After all, isn't man evolving into a better state? Doesn't all our "I'm okay, you're okay" positive self-image training work? Isn't man's problem just low self-esteem that leads to aberrant behavior? Isn't the solution more education so man can self-actualize?

In Ephesians 2:1–10 the Bible explains what's wrong with man. No passage in the New Testament reveals man's spiritual problem more clearly or explains more concisely what must be done for it to be removed. In this lesson you'll learn man has only one hope to overcome his sinful state and escape God's eternal judgment.

Now ask God to reveal Jesus Christ to you and to transform you into His image.

Focus Rule:

If the leader helps the group members focus on the Bible, they will gain confidence to study God's Word on their own.

ADD GROUP INSIGHTS BELOW

1. The question about man's nature is one of the greatest questions in life. Is man innately good, or is he inherently sinful and evil? If man is basically good, then aberrant

ADDITIONAL INSIGHTS

behavior must be met with better education, increased positive reinforcement, and more enlightenment of his latent goodness. On the other hand, if man is inherently sinful, then something must be done to rescue him from the temporal bondage and eternal consequences of his sinful nature. Do you believe man is inherently good or inherently sinful?

____

Why? ____

____

____

2. What is man's spiritual condition prior to salvation (Ephesians 2:1–2)?

____

____

____

____

3. Paul identifies with his readers (**we all once conducted ourselves**) when he describes man's nature prior to being saved (Ephesians 2:3). What three things does he say about himself and all mankind in relationship to sin and man's standing before God (Ephesians 2:3)?

We ____

____

We fulfilled ____________________________________

____

By nature, we were _______________________________

_______________________ just like everyone else.

4. Old Testament prophets Isaiah and Jeremiah described man's spiritual condition similarly, but they used different

imagery to help their audiences grasp the same truth about man's sinfulness.

a. What did Isaiah say to the people of his day about their spiritual condition, including his own (Isaiah 53:6; 64:6)?

1. ____
____(v. ____)

2. ____
____(v. ____)

b. What did Jeremiah say about man's nature (Jeremiah 17:9)?

____

____

c. How did Jesus describe man's spiritual condition (Matthew 7:11)?

____

____

d. What evidences do you see that man is inherently sinful and not just a victim of negative social influences?

____

____

____

____

5. The Bible's teaching about man's problem with sin brings us to a key question: "Is man a sinner because he sins, or does man sin because he is a sinner?" What do you think is the correct answer to this question? Why?

____

____

Drawing Rule:

To learn how to draw everyone into the group discussion without calling on anyone, go to www.LamplightersUSA.org/training.

ADDITIONAL INSIGHTS

ADDITIONAL INSIGHTS

6. In Ephesians 2:4 the words **But God** explode onto the scene and interrupt the narrative. Man, lost in sin and utterly helpless to save himself (Jeremiah 17:9; Romans 5:8), is offered a spiritual lifeline. God, and God alone, offers man the only means of deliverance from the penalty of sin (God's wrath) through faith in Jesus Christ.

   a. What does the Bible say about God's character that moves Him to extend His saving grace to man (Ephesians 2:4)?

      1.

      2.

   b. The timing of God's plan to rescue man is crucial to an understanding of grace. When did God make provision for the believer's salvation (Ephesians 2:4–6)?

   c. Why is the timing of God's provision for man's salvation so important?

7. The Bible uses the word **grace** to describe God's unconditional gift of eternal life to undeserving man. The famous hymn writer, John Newton, wrote these memorable

words that capture God's grace being extended to sinful man: *"Amazing grace! How sweet the sound that saved a wretch like me! I once was lost, but now am found; was blind, but now I see."*

Has your group become a "Holy huddle?" Learn how to reach out to others by taking online leadership training.

ADDITIONAL INSIGHTS

a. Man's salvation means more than simply being delivered from God's wrath. What else does God do for those who are redeemed?

   1. Ephesians 2:6: ______________________________

   ____

   2. 2 Corinthians 5:18: ______________________________

   ____

   3. Philippians 3:20: ______________________________

   ____

   4. 2 Corinthians 5:20: ______________________________

   ____

b. Ephesians 2:8–9 serves as a summary statement for God's benevolent acts of mercy and love. These verses teach several important truths about man's redemption. Please list four.

   1. ______________________________
   2. ______________________________
   3. ______________________________
   4. ______________________________

8. In Ephesians 2:10 the Bible says believers are **His** [God's] **workmanship**. The Greek word for workmanship (*poiema*) means a work of art or masterpiece. It is not the same Greek word as the one in Ephesians 2:9 which refers to man's work. Believers are God's masterpiece or work of art (from start [salvation] to finish) created in Christ Jesus. The believers' works don't save them or keep them because these works are prepared beforehand by God (Ephesians

ADDITIONAL INSIGHTS

2:9–10). What do you think these works are that God has prepared beforehand?

9. The word **walk** (Ephesians 2:10; NIV: "for us to do") provides an important clue regarding the nature of the works God wants believers to do. The purpose of these prepared-in-advance works is not to "work in them" but to **walk in them** as the Bible indicates. Believers are God's workmanship in salvation, sanctification, and service. Therefore, it is God who works in and through believers for His good pleasure.

   a. What do you think is the difference between (1) a believer working to do good works for God, even as an expression of gratitude for what God has done for him or her, and (2) a believer walking in the good works that God had prepared beforehand for him or her to do?

   b. Now examine your relationship with Christ. Would you describe it as (1) a crawl in which not much progress is being made, (2) a spiritual relay race with intermittent periods of waiting (no spiritual progress) followed by brief periods of (spiritual) exertion, or (3) a steady, deliberate walk with Christ toward spiritual maturity? Why?

Four

Temple of God

Read Ephesians 2:11–22; other references as given.

In the previous lesson you learned man's problem was not poor social engineering, low self-esteem, or even a lack of educational enlightenment. Man's problem is systemic, not symptomatic or environmental. Man's sin problem lies at the heart level. Man doesn't need a religious checkup. He needs a (spiritual) heart transplant. And only God can change a man's heart.

In Ephesians 2:11–22 you'll be introduced to a second aspect of God's master plan. Only after man is individually reconciled to God can he be reconciled to others, both ethnically and socially. All the international peace treaties will eventually fail unless man is first reconciled to God. In this lesson you'll learn how God reconciled two historically factious groups, Jews and Gentiles, and joined them into a new spiritual temple.

Before you begin this lesson, ask God to reveal Jesus Christ to you and to transform you into His image.

Gospel Gold Rule:

Try to get all the answers to the questions—not just the easy ones. Go for the gold.

ADD GROUP INSIGHTS BELOW

1. In Ephesians 2:11 there is a major change in subject. From the subject of God's plan for personal reconciliation (Ephesians 1:3–2:10), the focus shifts to group or ethnic reconciliation (Ephesians 2:11–3:21).

   a. Who does Paul address as his new audience in Ephesians 2:11–14?

   ____

ADDITIONAL INSIGHTS

b. What were Gentiles (non-Jews) called by Jews at that time (Ephesians 2:11)?

____

2. a. List five spiritual characteristics of all Gentile believers before they are saved (Ephesians 2:12).

1. ______________________________

____

2. ______________________________

____

3. ______________________________

____

4. ______________________________

____

5. ______________________________

____

b. Do you think these five characteristics are true of all unsaved people today, including those who are religious and have a general belief in God? Why?

____

____

____

c. Paul said the unsaved are **without hope** (Ephesians 2:12 NIV). The Bible expands this truth by saying that they are without hope in the world. What evidence do you see of unsaved people having no hope in this world?

____

____

____

3. What must happen to an unsaved person who has no personal relationship with Christ, is excluded from God's chosen people, is estranged from God's promises, has no hope (assurance) of an eternal union with God, and is without God in this world (Ephesians 2:13)?

____

____

4. If an individual is not redeemed, he or she is by nature a **son of disobedience** and a **child of** [God's] **wrath** (Ephesians 2:2–3). What replaces God's wrath in the life of a new believer (Ephesians 2:14–15; Romans 5:1)?

____

____

5. After God reconciled individual believing Jews and believing Gentiles to Himself through salvation in Jesus Christ, He joined them into one new body (Ephesians 2:14–16). How did Jesus reconcile the two groups and bridge this great ethnic divide?

____

____

6. The **middle wall of separation** (Ephesians 2:14; NIV: "the dividing wall") that originally separated Jews and Gentiles has been the subject of much debate. Various interpretations include: (1) the wall between the Court of the Gentiles and the inner temple in Jerusalem, (2) the curtain in the Jerusalem temple that separated the Holy Place from the Holy of Holies, (3) the "fence" around the Law mentioned by some rabbis, and (4) the spiritual enmity that historically has existed between Jews and Gentiles. What do you think Paul was referring to by this **wall of separation**?

____

____

Balance Rule:

To learn how to balance the group discussion, go to www.LamplightersUSA.org/training.

ADDITIONAL INSIGHTS

ADDITIONAL INSIGHTS

7. Throughout Ephesians chapter 2, Paul highlighted the spiritual benefits of the believer's union with Christ by contrasting man's former (unsaved) condition to his new (saved) standing in Christ. Complete the following chart by contrasting the spiritual condition of the non-redeemed to the new spiritual standing of believers before God.

Non-Christians are ...	Believers are/have ...
Dead in trespasses and sins (vv. 1, 5)	(v. 5)
Not saved by their works (v. 9)	(v. 8)
Aliens and strangers to God and His promises (v. 12)	(v. 19)
Have no hope (v. 12)	(vs. 14, 16)
Without (access to) God in this world (v. 12)	(v. 18)
Far off (from God) (v. 13)	(v. 19)

8. What names are used to describe this new union of believing Jews and Gentiles in one new body?

   1. Ephesians 2:19: __________

   2. Ephesians 2:21: __________

3. Ephesians 2:22: ______________________________

____

4. Ephesians 3:21: ______________________________

____

9. God made careful plans for the construction of His holy spiritual temple. Construction of ancient buildings, including the Egyptian pyramids, began with the laying of a cornerstone from which the remainder of the edifice was built. In Paul's illustration of the new holy temple of God, who do the following parts represent?

   a. The cornerstone: ______________________________

   ______________________________ (v. ____)

   b. The foundation: ______________________________

   ______________________________ (v. ____)

   c. The actual building/stones (1 Peter 2:4-5) __________

   ______________________________ (v. ____)

10. How does the Bible describe the ongoing construction of this spiritual temple that God is building as individuals are added to it through salvation (1 Corinthians 12:18; Ephesians 2:21–22; 1 Peter 2:5)?

____

______________________________ (__________)

____

______________________________ (__________)

____

______________________________ (__________)

____

______________________________ (__________)

Did you know Lamplighters is more than a small group ministry? It is a discipleship training ministry that uses a small group format to train disciple-makers. If every group trained one person per study, God would use these new disciple-makers to reach more people for Christ.

ADDITIONAL INSIGHTS

ADDITIONAL INSIGHTS

11. If you are a Christian, it pleased God to set you as a living stone into His new temple. Now you are part of a royal priesthood that offers spiritual sacrifices to God. How has this glorious truth impacted your life?

Five

A Great Mystery Revealed

Read Ephesians 3; other references as given.

In the last lesson you learned the second important aspect of God's master plan—the ingathering of believing Jews and Gentiles into one new spiritual temple of God. This gathering was an integral part of God's plan of bringing everything together under the sovereign authority of Jesus Christ (Ephesians 2:11). Gentile Christians are no longer aliens and strangers to God and His promises. They are fellow citizens and full members with believing Jews in God's family.

In Ephesians 3:1 Paul begins to pray that believing Jews and believing Gentiles would understand this truth, but the Holy Spirit redirects him to explain a great mystery that was hidden in ages past (Ephesians 3:2–13). In Ephesians 3:14–21 Paul returns to his prayer for believing Jews and Gentiles to fully comprehend God's marvelous plan and to embrace His amazing love that brought about this unlikely reconciliation of Jews and Gentiles. In this lesson you'll learn another aspect of God's master plan.

Before you begin, ask God to reveal Jesus Christ and to transform you into His image.

No-Trespassing Rule:

To keep the Bible study on track, avoid talking about political parties, church denominations, and Bible translations.

ADD GROUP INSIGHTS BELOW

1. In Ephesians 1:15 Paul used the words **Therefore I also** to alert his readers of another change in subject from theological truth to practical application. In Ephesians 3:1 he used similar words **For this reason I** to accomplish the same purpose and introduce his second prayer. Notice Paul doesn't actually return to his prayer until Ephesians 3:14

ADDITIONAL INSIGHTS

when he writes, **For this reason I bow my knees**. What was so important that the Holy Spirit redirected Paul from writing about praying for the Ephesians (Ephesians 3:3–4, 9)?

____

____

____

____

2. In the Bible, the Greek word for **mystery** (*musterion*) means "a truth hidden that is now revealed (by God)." The Greek meaning of the word is dissimilar to the English word for mystery which means "something that remains unknown or is unknowable."

   a. How did Paul come to understand this great mystery (Ephesians 3:3, 5)?

   ____

   ____

   b. Paul regarded the truth God revealed to him as a solemn stewardship or dispensation (Ephesians 3:2). At the end of his life he was able to testify that he'd been a faithful servant to God. What three things did Paul say about his own faithfulness to the truth God revealed to him (2 Timothy 4:7)?

   1. _______________

   ____

   2. _______________

   ____

   3. _______________

   ____

3. God has commissioned every believer to be His steward and guardian of the truth (Jude 3). In what ways do you,

like Paul, fight the good fight (for the truth) and stand for the truth in your family, workplace, and community?

4. Paul said he had already written briefly about God's great mystery (Ephesians 3:3; 2:11–22). This mystery had not been revealed in the past but had been revealed to the apostles and the (New Testament) prophets (Ephesians 3:5). Do you think this great mystery was (1) that God had included the Gentiles in His plan, (2) that Gentiles could be saved, (3) that Gentiles were given equal status within His great plan of cosmic reconciliation, or (4) something else? Why?

5. Some Bible teachers believe that God's great mystery of gathering believing Jews and Gentiles into one great household as equal members replaces the promises He originally gave to national Israel. According to this view, all yet-to-be-fulfilled promises God made to national Israel will now be fulfilled within the church. According to this view, there will be no future restoration of national Israel, and all the prophetic passages that deal with national Israel's future should be interpreted figuratively. Do you think the gathering of believing Jews and believing Gentiles into this new spiritual temple of God invalidates or nullifies His original promises to national Israel (Romans 11:29; Titus 1:2)? Why?

If you use table tents or name tags, it will help visitors feel more comfortable and new members will be assimilated more easily into your group.

ADDITIONAL INSIGHTS

ADDITIONAL INSIGHTS

____

____

6. Some people believe God can do anything, but as Titus 1:2 states, God cannot lie. List four additional things God cannot do (2 Timothy 2:13; Hebrews 13:8, James 1:13)?

   1. ______________________________
      ______________________ (__________)
   2. ______________________________
      ______________________ (__________)
   3. ______________________________
      ______________________ (__________)
   4. ______________________________
      ______________________ (__________)

7. Because God cannot lie, His Word is true, His promises are sure, and His judgments are certain. What promises in God's Word are your greatest comfort and encouragement? Why?

____

____

____

____

____

8. Some Christians believe God's master plan is simply seeing the lost come to Christ and for them to live happier ever after in heaven. Others believe that God saves the lost, both Jews and Gentiles, and joins them in one glorious body, the household of God, that will eventually be transported to heaven. But God's master plan is much greater than that. In Ephesians 3:9–11 Paul expands on God's master

plan that was first introduced in Ephesians 1:9–10. Explain God's master plan in the fullest sense in your own words (Ephesians 3:9–11).

Use the side margins to write down spiritual insights from other people in your group. Add the person's name and the date to help you remember in the future.

ADDITIONAL INSIGHTS

9. If the church doesn't understand God's master plan, it can easily fall prey to the "people and programs" syndrome or become focused on the "four Bs" (bodies, buildings, budgets, and busyness).

   a. When a church loses sight of God's glorious calling to manifest God's glory, wisdom, and love, it can quickly forsake its true calling from God and become institutionalized. What do you think the church of Jesus Christ can do to manifest God's glory, wisdom, and love to a lost world to a greater extent?

make known

   b. If you are a Christian, what do you think you can do to better demonstrate God's glory and will through your life?

ADDITIONAL INSIGHTS

c. What was Paul's response when he reflected on God's master plan for His church and this world (Ephesians 3:14, 17–19)?

____

____

____

____

10. In Ephesians 3:14–19 Paul prays for four things for the Ephesians that every Christian would be wise to pray for on behalf of other believers. List these four things Paul prayed God would give the Ephesians.

1. ____
______________________________________ (v. _____)

2. ____
______________________________________ (v. _____)

3. ____
______________________________________ (v. _____)

4. ____
______________________________________ (v. _____)

11. Ephesians 3 concludes with a doxology, which is a prayer of praise and adoration to God for who He is and what He does (Ephesians 3:20–21). What does the Bible teach you about God and His greatness in this doxology?

____

____

____

____

SIX

WORTHY OF GOD'S CALLING

Read Ephesians 4:1–16; other references as given.

In Ephesians chapters 1–3, Paul explained two important aspects of God's master plan: (1) God's plan of redemption and (2) the establishment of the new holy temple of God in which believing Jews and Gentiles are equal members.

Beginning in Ephesians chapter 4, the Bible instructs believers how they can participate fully in God's master plan. Every believer has been placed in the body of Christ as it pleased God (1 Corinthians 12:18), and each member has been personally invited to join Him in building His glorious temple (Ephesians 2:20–22, 1 Corinthians 3:9-12).

In Ephesians 4:1–6 the Bible emphasizes the importance of spiritual unity within the body of Christ. In Ephesians 4:7–16 Paul emphasizes the uniqueness of some spiritual gifts and how they are to be used to build up the body of Christ. In this lesson you'll learn how God wants to use you to accomplish His grand plan of gathering everything under the sovereign authority of Jesus Christ.

Now ask God to reveal Jesus Christ to you and to transform you into the image of His Son.

Transformation Rule:

Seek for personal transformation, not mere information, from God's Word.

ADD GROUP INSIGHTS BELOW

1. In the first three chapters of Ephesians, one of the main emphases is on the *wealth* of the believer (the riches of Christ, Ephesians 1:7, 18; 2:7; 3:8). In the last three chapters the key emphasis is on the *walk* of the believer (Ephesians 4:1, 17; 5:2, 8, 15).

ADDITIONAL INSIGHTS

a. In light of Ephesians 1–3, what do you think it means for a Christian **to walk worthy of the calling with which you were called** (Ephesians 4:1; 3:8-11; NIV: "live a life worthy of [your] calling")?

b. Why do you think Paul identifies himself as **a prisoner of the Lord** at this point in the letter?

2. The first command in Ephesians focuses the believer's attention on being, rather than doing. Instead of encouraging his readers to do some noble act of Christian service in God's name, Paul implores them to fully embrace the person and character of Jesus Christ.

   a. In your own words describe the Christlike attitudes God expects His followers to exhibit—attributes that demonstrate they are willing to walk worthy of their high calling in Jesus Christ (Ephesians 4:2).

   b. Believers don't need to produce spiritual unity with other believers. They should, however, endeavor to keep or preserve the unity of the Spirit as equal fellow-members of God's family (Ephesians 4:3). What are some things

Christians do that hinder and destroy spiritual unity among God's people (Ephesians 4:25; 29, 31; Proverbs 10:18)?

1. ______________________________
______________________________ (________)

2. ______________________________
______________________________ (________)

3. ______________________________
______________________________ (________)

4. ______________________________
______________________________ (________)

3. Christians can be united in the faith because they have six things in common (Ephesians 4:4–6). Try to identify these six commonalities.

one body ______________________________

one Spirit ______________________________

one hope ______________________________
____

one Lord ______________________________

one faith ______________________________
____

one baptism ______________________________
____

4. Many liberal churches and denominations have sought to promote spiritual unity at the expense of denying fundamental doctrines of the Christian faith. The modern ecumenical movement (National Council of Churches, World Council of Churches) with its "Let's not get hung up on Bible doctrine; let's just love one another" philosophy has routinely forsaken doctrines such as the inerrancy of the Bible, the sinlessness

Would you like to learn how to prepare a life-changing Bible study using a simple 4-step process? Contact Lamplighters and ask about ST-A-R-T.

ADDITIONAL INSIGHTS

ADDITIONAL INSIGHTS

of Christ, salvation through Christ alone through faith alone, the physical return of Christ, and the bodily resurrection of the believer. In your opinion, how can a Christian can keep the unity of the faith without compromising the truth?

____

____

____

5. Beginning in Ephesians 4:7, Paul transitions from teaching about genuine spiritual unity to the importance of certain spiritual gifts and ministries within the body of Christ. Every Christian is given at least one spiritual gift according to Christ's choosing (Ephesians 4:7). Jesus also gave **some to be apostles, some prophets, some evangelists, and some pastors and teachers** (Ephesians 4:11). Jesus Christ is the cornerstone, and the apostles and prophets served as the original foundation of the early church and provided the church with New Testament revelation (Ephesians 2:20). Evangelists are spiritually gifted individuals who do missionary work and seek to establish new churches. In the Greek New Testament, the phrase *pastors and teachers* can be understood either as a single gift (pastor/teacher) or as two people gifts (pastors and teachers).

   a. Why did Jesus Christ give these "gifts" to the church (Ephesians 4:12)?

   ____

   ____

   ____

   b. Who and what does the edifying of the body of Christ (Ephesians 4:11–12; 1 Corinthians 3:5–7; Hebrews 12:1–3)? Be careful when you answer this question. The answer may not be as simple as it seems.

   ____

   ____

____

____

____

6. When will this ministry of edifying (the building up in the faith) the body of Christ be completed (Ephesians 4:13)?

____

____

____

7. No believer will ever reach a state of sinlessness (1 John 1:8), but he or she can become spiritually mature in Christ (Ephesians 4:13). What are some indications that a believer has not reached spiritual maturity (Ephesians 4:14; Hebrews 5:11–12)?

____

____

____

____

____

____

8. God give some believers specific spiritual gifts so they can serve and equip His church (Ephesians 4:11). These spiritual leaders are to equip the body of Christ for the work of the ministry (Ephesians 4:12).

   a. Many spiritual leaders believe the preaching and teaching of God's Word during the weekly services of the church is sufficient to equip God's people for ministry. According to a national survey, however, only 5 percent of adult Christians have ever led another adult to a saving faith in Jesus Christ. Besides preaching to the multitudes (Matthew 4:23; 9:35), what else did Jesus

If the leader places a watch on the table, participants will feel confident that the Bible study will be completed on time. If the leader doesn't complete the lesson each week, participants will be less likely to do their weekly lessons, and the discussion will not be as rich.

ADDITIONAL INSIGHTS

ADDITIONAL INSIGHTS

do to equip His followers for effective ministry (Mark 1:17)?

____

____

____

____

b. Many Christians believe Christ's command to make disciples (often called the Great Commission) includes a mandate to teach all nations (Matthew 28:18–20). Upon closer examination of Matthew 28:20 the Bible actually says **teaching them to observe all things that I have commanded you.** What do you think is the difference, if any, between teaching them (all nations), and teaching them to observe all things?

____

____

____

____

____

____

9. List several spiritual benefits that will occur when spiritual leaders equip (not just teach but train) the saints for the work of the ministry, and believers do that work (Ephesians 4:13–16).

1. ____

_______________________________________ (v. _____)

2. ____

_______________________________________ (v. _____)

3. ____

_______________________________________ (v. _____)

ADDITIONAL INSIGHTS

4. ____

______________________________________ (v. _____)

5. ____

______________________________________ (v. _____)

6. ____

______________________________________ (v. _____)

ADDITIONAL INSIGHTS

Seven

The New Man

Read Ephesians 4:17–32; other references as given.

In the previous lesson you learned that Christians participate in God's master plan when they live worthy of their high calling in Christ. To do this, they must live in unity with other members of the body of Christ and use their spiritual gifts to glorify God and build up the body of Christ. Spiritual leaders must go beyond teaching believers and train them to observe all things Jesus commanded.

In Ephesians 4:17–32 you'll learn about the second "walk" of the believer. Christians must put off the old life of sin and self-deception and put on the new man in Christ.

Now ask God to reveal Jesus Christ and to transform you into His image.

If the leader asks all the study questions, the group discussion will be more likely to stay on track.

ADD GROUP INSIGHTS BELOW

1. a. What do you think it means to **no longer walk as the rest of the Gentiles walk** (Ephesians 4:17; NIV: "no longer live as the Gentiles do")?

   ____

   ____

   b. The Bible says that the Gentiles (in these verses, unsaved persons rather than non-Jews) live in the emptiness or futility of their minds (Ephesians 4:17). List six results of this reality in the lives of unsaved people (Ephesians 4:18–19).

ADDITIONAL INSIGHTS

1. ______________________________ (v. ____)
2. ______________________________ (v. ____)
3. ______________________________ (v. ____)
4. ______________________________ (v. ____)
5. ______________________________ (v. ____)
6. ______________________________ (v. ____)

2. The first words in Ephesians 4:20, **But you,** are reminiscent of the words **But God** in Ephesians 2:4 and **But now** in Ephesians 2:13. In all three instances God intervenes to rescue man from self-destruction and provides him with the way of escape. What must take place in a Christian's life so he stops living like an unsaved person in the futility (emptiness) of his mind (Ephesians 4:20–24)?

____

____

____

____

____

3. The spiritual concept of "putting off" and "putting on" (Ephesians 4:22, 24) emphasizes the believer's responsibility to make righteous choices that will positively affect his or her walk with Christ. In salvation the believer is the recipient of God's grace (this is called the *passive voice* in the Greek language: "You have been saved") (Ephesians 2:8).

Regarding progressive sanctification (spiritual growth), the believer participates with the Holy Spirit in his or her own spiritual maturation (this is called the *middle voice* in the Greek language: "The boy hit himself").

a. Some Christians try to put off their sinful ways by exerting self-determination or exercising rigorous personal discipline. They find out quickly that this doesn't work (Romans 7:18–24; Colossians 2:20–23). If self-determination and personal discipline are ineffective to overcome sin, how does a Christian fulfill the command to put off the old sin nature (2 Corinthians 10:4–5; Galatians 5:16–18)?

____

____

____

____

b. If you are a Christian, in what ways are you actively putting off your old sinful habits and putting on the new man in Christ?

____

____

____

____

c. If God commands believers to put off the old man (their sinful nature) and gives them the power to do this, do you think they can get to a place of spiritual maturity where they are no longer tempted to sin? Why?

____

____

____

____

The Bible says, *So then faith comes by hearing and hearing by the word of God* (Romans 10:17). Every time you humbly study God's Word, your faith grows.

ADDITIONAL INSIGHTS

ADDITIONAL INSIGHTS

4. The spiritual concept of "putting off" and "putting on" also emphasizes the need for radical, spiritual transformation. Both phrases indicate an urgency for believers to rid themselves of everything that defiles and embrace everything that pleases Christ.

   a. The apostle Matthew was a tax gatherer (lower level tax collector) when Jesus called him to be one of His disciples. When and how did Matthew respond to Jesus' call (Matthew 9:9)?

   ____

   ____

   b. When did Jesus expect the woman caught in adultery to "put off" her old ways of immoral conduct (John 8:3–11)?

   ____

   ____

   ____

   ____

   ____

   c. Is there something (sin, habit, attitude, etc.) in your life that you need to put off—something you know is displeasing to God? When do you think you should obey God?

   ____

   ____

   ____

   ____

   ____

5. In Ephesians 4:25–29 there are four exhortations. Each exhortation has three parts: (1) a negative command, (2)

a positive command, and (3) the reason for adopting the positive command. In the second one (Ephesians 4:26–27) the order of the first two parts is reversed. Identify the various elements in each exhortation. You will need to put the second exhortation in your own words to answer the question.

a. Ephesians 4:25:

1. Don't ______________________________

2. Do ______________________________

3. Why? ______________________________

____

b. Ephesians 4:26–27:

1. Be ______________________________

2. But don't ______________________________

3. Why? ______________________________

____

c. Ephesians 4:28:

1. Don't ______________________________

2. Do ______________________________

3. Why? ______________________________

____

d. Ephesians 4:29:

1. Don't ______________________________

2. Do ______________________________

3. Why? ______________________________

____

It's a good time to begin praying and inviting new people for your next Open House.

ADDITIONAL INSIGHTS

ADDITIONAL INSIGHTS

6. What do you think it means to grieve the Holy Spirit (Ephesians 4:30; James 4:5)?

7. If a Christian is going to work with God to accomplish His grand plan, what sinful habits and actions as well as ungodly speech patterns should he put off (Ephesians 4:31)?

8. Sometimes Christians find it hard to forgive others even though God has commanded them to do so. What spiritual truth must a Christian remember when he or she is attempting to forgive those who have sinned against them (Ephesians 4:32)?

9. What did you learn in this passage of Scripture that will change your life forever?

Eight

Imitators of God

Read Ephesians 5:1–21; other references as given.

In the last lesson you learned about becoming a new man in Christ. The Bible says **If anyone is in Christ, he is a new creation; old things have passed away; behold, all things have become new** (2 Corinthians 5:17). But even though the Christian has become a new creation at salvation, he or she must still "put off" the old man and "put on" the new man in Christ to walk worthy of God's calling.

In Ephesians 5:1–21 Paul exhorts his readers to become imitators of God. Having already instructed them to walk worthy of the Lord and to walk no longer as the Gentiles, Paul adds two more "walk" exhortations—to **walk in love** (Ephesians 5:2) and to **walk as children of light** (Ephesians 5:8). In this lesson you'll learn the consequences of walking in darkness and the importance of walking in the light.

Before you begin, ask God to reveal Jesus Christ to you and to transform you into His image.

Is your study going well? Consider starting a new group. To learn how, go to www.LamplightersUSA.org/training.

ADD GROUP INSIGHTS BELOW

1. a. To be an imitator of someone else means you mimic their manner of speech and the things they do. What do you think it means to become an imitator of God?

____

____

____

ADDITIONAL INSIGHTS

b. In which of the following areas of your life are you *intentionally* imitating God? Circle your answers.

Speech	Life Purpose	Sacrifice
Associations	Loving others	Moral Purity
Forgiving Others	Grace	Patience
Resisting Sin	Truth	Honesty
Humility		

2. Jesus Christ is God in the flesh (God incarnate). He was not created; He is not a lesser God; He did not become God when He was resurrected; He is the eternal God. The writer of Hebrews says God **has in these last days spoken to us by His Son, whom He has appointed heir of all things, through whom also He made the worlds; who being the brightness of His glory and the express image of His person, and upholding all things by the word of His power, when He had by Himself** [J B Phillips: "in person"] **purged our sins, sat down at the right hand of the Majesty on high** (Hebrews 1:2–3).

   a. The Bible says Jesus is the express or exact image (Gk. *eikon*) of God, the Father. How did Jesus Christ imitate the Father when He lived on earth (Ephesians 5:2; John 8:29; 17:4, 26)?

   ____

   ____

   ____

   ____

   ____

   b. How did the Father regard Jesus' obedience and willingness to honor Him (Ephesians 5:2)?

   ____

   ____

c. How does God regard believers who are obedient to Him (2 Corinthians 2:15)?

____

____

3. List the six sins that should have no place in the lives of God's people (Ephesians 5:3–4).

1. ______________________________________ (v. ____)
2. ______________________________________ (v. ____)
3. ______________________________________ (v. ____)
4. ______________________________________ (v. ____)
5. ______________________________________ (v. ____)
6. ______________________________________ (v. ____)

4. How do you think Christians can fulfill the command of separating from all sin without coming across as spiritually arrogant or being "holier than thou" to unsaved friends—the very people that Christ died for and God commands them to reach with the message of salvation (1 Corinthians 5:9–10)?

____

____

____

____

____

____

____

5. The Bible says that no **fornicator, unclean** [sexually impure] **person, nor covetous man … has any inheritance in the kingdom of Christ and God** (Ephesians 5:5). Initially the inclusion of covetousness with the list of sexual sins of fornication and uncleanness seems out of place.

It's time to choose your next study. Turn to the back of the study guide for a list of available studies or go online for the latest studies.

ADDITIONAL INSIGHTS

ADDITIONAL INSIGHTS

a. What characteristics do you think **fornication** and **covetousness** have in common?

____

____

____

____

____

b. What specifically do you think is referred to by **uncleanness** (Ephesians 5:3; NIV: "impurity")?

____

____

____

6. What does the Bible teach about the fate of those who persist in living in fornication, sexual impurity, or covetousness (Ephesians 5:5; Revelation 21:8)?

____

____

____

7. Christians should not dismiss or discount the seriousness of God's commands to be morally pure and to refrain from coveting (Ephesians 5:5; NIV: "greedy"). Nor should believers think God will not judge sexual misconduct. Statements like "I wouldn't marry someone I haven't slept with before marriage. How would we know if we are compatible?" and "We don't need a piece of paper to be married—we're in a committed relationship" are examples of individuals who are rationalizing their sin.

   a. What are some other statements you have heard people say to justify their sexual sin—statements that are contrary to God's standard of moral purity?

1. ______________________

2. ______________________

3. ______________________

4. ______________________

b. If you are a Christian, you are called to be an imitator of God (Ephesians 5:1). Are you imitating God in the area of moral behavior? Yes / No

If not, why? ______________________

____

____

8. Why should all believers live distinctively Christian lives (Ephesians 5:8–9)?

____

____

____

____

9. Rather than living in sin and reaping its painful consequences (loss of fellowship with God, troubled conscience, guilt, [Holy Spirit] conviction, broken relationships, emotional pain, etc.), God's people should live as **children of light** (Ephesians 5:8). One pastor said, "I can never understand why so many Christians fight so hard to keep doing the things that God saved them from."

a. Instead of justifying sinful behavior, believers are commanded to have **no fellowship with the works of darkness, but rather expose them** (Ephesians 5:11–12). If believers are commanded not to judge nonbelievers (1 Corinthians 5:9–13), how can a believer fulfill this command (Matthew 18:15–18, Galatians 6:1)?

____

You can be trained to fulfill the Great Commission. You can take the first step by taking Level 1 (Basic Training), using the student workbook in the back of this study guide. You can take the training individually or as a group.

ADDITIONAL INSIGHTS

ADDITIONAL INSIGHTS

____

____

____

____

b. Believers are to wake up (spiritually) and let the light of God's truth shine in them and through their lives rather than engaging in a host of sinful behaviors (the deeds of the old man; Galatians 5:19–21). List three things you can do to live a God-honoring life (Ephesians 5:15–17).

1. _______________

_______________ (_______)

2. _______________

_______________ (_______)

3. _______________

_______________ (_______)

10. Paul compares two unlikely things to illustrate what it means to be filled with the Holy Spirit (Ephesians 5:18). Rather than being drunk (filled) with wine, believers are commanded to be filled with the Holy Spirit.

a. All believers are washed or baptized by the Holy Spirit at the time of salvation as they are placed into Christ (Romans 8:9; 1 Corinthians 12:13; Titus 3:5). They are also sealed by the Spirit, whose presence in the believer's life is God's guarantee of their future redemption (Ephesians 1:13–14). Believers are not commanded to be baptized or sealed in the Spirit, but they are commanded to be filled with the Spirit (Ephesians 5:18). What *do you think* it means to be filled with the Spirit?

____

____

____

ADDITIONAL INSIGHTS

____

b. List three evidences that a person is filled with the Spirit (Ephesians 5:19–21)? Please put your answer in your own words.

1. ______________________________________
   ____
   ____________________________(__________)

2. ______________________________________
   ____
   ____________________________(__________)

3. ______________________________________
   ____
   ____________________________(__________)

11. What did you learn in this lesson that will help you become an imitator of God?

____

____

____

____

____

____

____

ADDITIONAL INSIGHTS

NINE

SPIRIT-FILLED LIVING

Read Ephesians 5:22–6:9; other references as given.

In the last lesson you learned that you are to be an imitator of God. Born into God's family through saving faith in Christ, every believer should bear a distinctive, family resemblance. The Christian's life, once marked by sexual sin, uncleanness, and covetousness, should now to be marked with goodness, righteousness, and truth. To imitate God, believers must live circumspectly, know God's will, and be filled with the Holy Spirit.

In Ephesians 5:22–6:9 Paul applies the command to be imitators of God to the home (Ephesians 5:22–6:4) and workplace (Ephesians 6:5–9). In this study you'll learn that God's master plan includes the Christian's closest human relationships (marriage, family) and one of the greatest venues for missionary outreach (the workplace). Both opportunities must be yielded to God if the believer expects to walk worthy of His calling.

Now ask God to reveal Jesus Christ and to transform you into His image.

Many groups study the Final Exam the week after the final lesson for three reasons: (1) someone might come to Christ, (2) believers gain assurance of salvation, (3) group members learn how to share the gospel.

ADD GROUP INSIGHTS BELOW

1. In Ephesians 5:18–21 the Bible teaches that one indication of being filled with the Spirit is a willingness to submit to one another in the fear of the God (Ephesians 5:21). Spirit-filled submission doesn't mean capitulating to every expression of ungodly dictatorship. It means having an attitude of "entreatability" or a willingness to yield (James 3:17) that is born in submission to God and His word, and a sensitivity to the Holy Spirit's leading.

ADDITIONAL INSIGHTS

a. How does a godly Christian woman demonstrate that she is filled with the Spirit in her relationship to her husband (Ephesians 5:22–33)?

b. How does a godly Christian man demonstrate that he is filled with the Spirit in his relationship with his wife (Ephesians 5:21, 25, 28, 33)?

c. Why do you think the command for husbands to love their wives is repeated three times in this passage?

2. The biblical teaching on male headship is rejected by some as being chauvinistic and archaic. The word *chauvinism* derives its name from a Napoleonic soldier named Nicolas Chauvin. Originally chauvinism was defined as an unwavering devotion and fanatical partiality to a group or cause to which one belongs. But it has come to refer to anyone whose partisanship includes prejudice against outsiders or members of the opposite sex, especially men. In what ways do you think the biblical teaching on male headship in the family and chauvinism are dissimilar?

____

____

3. a. The husband is commanded to love his wife **as Christ loved the church** (Ephesians 5:25). In what ways did Jesus love the church (Ephesians 5:25–27)?

____

____

____

____

____

b. In what specific ways do you think a Christian husband could love his wife **as Christ loved the church**?

____

____

____

____

4. A Christian husband is commanded to love his wife as Christ loved the church (Ephesians 5:25). The Bible uses two other comparisons to show the depth of Christlike love that a husband should have for his wife. Please identify them (Ephesians 5:25–33).

1. ____

____(v. _____)

2. ____

____(v. _____)

5. The phrase husbands ought to love their wives **as they do their own bodies** (Ephesians 5:28) seems to contradict the common counseling concept that teaches people must learn to love ourselves before we can love others. The

Having trouble with your group? A Lamplighters trainer can help you solve the problem.

ADDITIONAL INSIGHTS

ADDITIONAL INSIGHTS

problem, however, is not that we don't love ourselves; we love ourselves too much and love Christ too little. If the first command to husbands (to love our wives as Christ loved the church) teaches the need for sacrificial love, what do you think the command for husbands to love their wives as they should love their own bodies teaches (Ephesians 5:29–31)?

____

____

____

____

____

6. a. If you are a married man, what could you do to love your wife in a more God-honoring way? (Women): What biblical advice would you give a young man who asked you how should he love his wife in a God-honoring way?

____

____

____

____

b. If a husband is not loving his wife in a Christlike manner or is disobeying the Lord in other ways, what should she do to honor God and win her husband to righteous behavior (Ephesians 5:33; 1 Peter 3:1–4)?

____

____

____

____

7. In Ephesians 5:31 Paul quotes from Genesis 2:24 to provide additional instruction to husbands about how they can love their wives in a God-honoring way. Name three key truths

about marriage taught in this verse—truths that every married couple should accept (Ephesians 5:31).

1. ______________________________

____

2. ______________________________

____

3. ______________________________

____

8. What do you think is the great mystery that Paul refers to in Ephesians 5:32?

____

____

____

____

9. a. In Ephesians 6:1–4 the biblical teaching moves from the husband-wife relationship to the immediate family. In your opinion, how can a child walk worthy of the Lord (Ephesians 6:1–3)?

____

____

b. How can fathers and mothers parent their children in such a way that they do not become disheartened and provoked to anger (Ephesians 6:4)?

____

____

____

____

____

It's time to order your next study. Allow enough time to get the books so you can distribute them at the Open House. Consider ordering 2-3 extra books for newcomers.

ADDITIONAL INSIGHTS

ADDITIONAL INSIGHTS

10. Paul addresses the employee-employer relationship and the Christian's responsibility in the workplace. In the ancient Roman Empire there were approximately 40–50 million slaves. The word **slave** (Greek *doulos*) referred to anyone in an indentured position, including those who were given great responsibility of overseeing and managing entire households. Although the slave–master relationship was somewhat distinct from the modern employee–employer relationship, the comparison can be rightfully applied.

    a. How can a Christian employee acknowledge God's supremacy over his or her life (Ephesians 6:5–8)?

    ____

    ____

    ____

    ____

    ____

    b. How can a Christian employer acknowledge God's supremacy over his or her life (Ephesians 6:9)?

    ____

    ____

    ____

    ____

    ____

11. It must have been an interesting transition within the early church when new believers (slaves, masters) were making the transition from unrighteous (slothfulness, theft, etc.) to godly treatment of each other in the fear of the Lord. Perhaps there were new Christian employees (slaves) who asked forgiveness for their poor work performance or employers (masters) who asked forgiveness for having threatened their slaves and began to treat them fairly.

ADDITIONAL INSIGHTS

Maybe both slaves and masters even worshipped together in the same church.

a. If you are a Christian employee, do you strive to do your work with excellence and for God's glory? Do you see your workplace (home, school, job, etc.) as God's calling and as your opportunity to be His witness?

   Yes / No / Sometimes

   If not, what could you do differently to honor the Lord at work?

   ____

   ____

   ____

   ____

b. If you are an employer, do you lead with excellence and treat everyone fairly, knowing that God is your master and He is watching how you treat your employees?
   Yes / No / Sometimes
   If not, what could you do differently to honor the Lord at work?

   ____

   ____

   ____

   ____

ADDITIONAL INSIGHTS

Ten

The Great Cosmic Conflict

Read Ephesians 6:10–24; other references as given.

In the last lesson you learned God's plan to bring all things under the sovereign authority of Jesus Christ including the believer's marriage, family, and work. Every Christian husband, wife, child, employee, and employer can express his or her devotion to Christ by living a Spirit-filled life.

Ephesians 6:10–24 describes a great cosmic conflict. All believers are conscripted into this great cosmic conflict at salvation. The battles in this epic conflict are fought against an invisible enemy using unconventional weapons. But even though the war is intense, victory is assured for the one who obeys his commanding officer (Jesus Christ).

In this lesson you'll learn many important truths about this great world war—truths found nowhere else in the Bible. You will also learn Christ's strategy that will enable you to be victorious.

Before you study this last lesson, ask God to reveal Jesus Christ and to transform you into His image.

Final Exam:

Are you meeting next week to study the Final Exam? To learn how to present it effectively, contact Lamplighters.

ADD GROUP INSIGHTS BELOW

1. a. Believers are commanded to **be strong in the Lord** so they can stand against the attacks of the devil (Ephesians 6:10). What do you think it means for a Christian to be strong in the Lord (Ephesians 6:10; Romans 4:20; 2 Timothy 2:1)?

____

____

ADDITIONAL INSIGHTS

b. List three specific things you are doing on a *daily* basis to be strengthened in your faith so you are prepared for the spiritual battles of life.

1. ______

2. ______

3. ______

2. a. The Bible exhorts believers to put on **the whole armor of God** (Ephesians 6:11, 13). What promise is given all those who put on the armor of God (Ephesians 6:11, 13, 16)?

b. Why do you think this promise is repeated three times in this passage?

3. You must know the enemy if you expect to be victorious in battle. Who or what are the believer's enemies in this great cosmic conflict (Ephesians 6:11–12, 16)?

4. a. If a believer puts on the whole armor of God, he or she will be **able to stand against the wiles of the devil** (Ephesians 6:11). The Greek word for **wiles** (*methodeai*) refers to the scheming, craftiness, methods, and

stratagems that the devil uses to deceive believers. Look at the following verses to identify some of the schemes or methods the devil uses to deceive believers.

1. Genesis 2:15–17; 3:1: ____________________

____

2. Genesis 3:3–4: ____________________

____

3. Genesis 3:5: ____________________

____

4. 2 Peter 2:1–2: ____________________

____

b. In 1 Timothy 3:7 and 2 Timothy 2:26 Paul uses the Greek word (*pagida*) for **snare** in both passages to emphasize the craftiness of Satan's methods. Study the following verses carefully and identify some of the snares or traps Satan uses to trap Christians.

1. Proverbs 1:10–19: ____________________

____

2. Proverbs 5:1–5: ____________________

____

3. Daniel 4:28–33: ____________________

____

4. Mark 7:9–13: ____________________

____

5. 1 Timothy 6:9: ____________________

____

c. What is the devil's goal or objective for your life (John 10:10; **the thief** in this verse is the devil)?

____

Would you like to learn how to lead someone through this same study? It's not hard. Go to www.LamplightersUSA.org to register for *free* online leadership training.

ADDITIONAL INSIGHTS

ADDITIONAL INSIGHTS

5. In Ephesians 6:10–20 Paul uses several military images (**armor, breastplate, shield, darts, helmet,** and **sword**) to depict the intensity of the believer's ongoing spiritual battle. In Ephesians 6:12, however, the apostle switches metaphors and says believers **do not wrestle against flesh and blood,** but against spiritual forces of darkness in the heavenlies (Ephesians 6:12). The Greek word for **wrestle** (*pale*) is both illustrative and instructive. In ancient times men fought intense wrestling matches for the entertainment of others. In what ways do you think the believer's struggle against the spiritual forces of darkness can be compared to a wrestling match?

6. The believer must put on the whole armor of God if he or she expects to stand firm (a term used of a soldier holding his ground, i.e., not retreating) against the wiles or schemes of the devil (Ephesians 6:11, 13). Try to identify each of the following pieces of armor that a Christian must put on to protect himself against the attack of the evil one. Note: Since these pieces of armor are "put on" by a believer, they don't refer to salvation.

   a. Waist girded with truth (v. 14): ______

   b. Breastplate of righteousness (v. 14): ______

c. Feet shod with the preparation of the gospel of peace (v. 15): ______________________

____

d. Shield of faith (v. 16): ______________________

____

e. Helmet of salvation (v. 17): ______________________

____

f. Sword of the Spirit (v. 17): ______________________

____

7. Some believers trivialize the reality of spiritual warfare while others become overly preoccupied with it. The former reduce spiritual warfare to a battle of the human will with victory being secured by personal discipline. The latter seem to believe Satan is preoccupied with their every move and responsible for all their trials and failures. What do you think is the proper biblical perspective regarding the Christian's spiritual battle with the forces of evil?

____

____

____

8. Paul concludes his letter to the Ephesians with a personal request for prayer (Ephesians 6:18–20) and some words of introduction and commendation of Tychicus, who was likely his letter carrier (Ephesians 6:21–22).

   a. What did Paul ask the Ephesians to pray on his behalf (Ephesians 6:18–20)?

   ____

   ____

   ____

For more discipleship help, sign up to receive the Disciple-Maker Tips—a bi-monthly email that provides insights to help your small group function more effectively.

ADDITIONAL INSIGHTS

ADDITIONAL INSIGHTS

b. If you are a Christian, does the spiritual condition of the lost (spiritually dead, without God, without hope, strangers to the covenants of promise) motivate you to beg God for boldness and to ask others to pray for you so you will share the gospel? Why?

____

____

____

____

9. What are the most significant truths you learned in your study of Ephesians?

1. ____

____

2. ____

____

3. ____

____

4. ____

____

10. Now that you have completed this study of Ephesians, do you think you could lead someone else or a small group through this same study if you received adequate leadership training?

Yes / No

Why? ____

____

____

____

LEADER'S GUIDE

Lesson 1: God's Master Plan

1. a. The book of Ephesians reveals God's master plan for His creation in this age and the age to come (Ephesians 1:9–11; 3:8–11). His master plan is to bring everything together under the sovereign authority of Christ—everything in heaven and on earth (Ephesians 1:10).
   b. 1. What in the world is God doing?
      2. Why am I here?

2. The word *saint* (Gk. *hagios*) is the normal designation for all New Testament believers. The word saint refers to all those who have placed their faith in Christ alone for eternal life and are now set apart by God for His service. In 1 Corinthians 1:2 Paul addresses the Corinthian believers as saints even though their spiritual conduct was worldly and ungodly (1 Corinthians 3:1-4). The apostle was referring to their position or standing in Christ, not the personal spiritual conduct.

3. a. In the Old Testament, the word shalom (peace) is one of the most significant terms and can be defined as "fulfillment, completion, maturity, soundness, wholeness, community, harmony, tranquility, security, welfare, friendship, agreement, success, and prosperity" (*International Standard Bible Encyclopedia*). Peace is often understood as the opposite of war (Ecclesiastes 3:8) and can also be used to describe the end of military conflict. Individually, the word peace stresses a state of serenity, either resulting from an absence of negative eternal circumstances or due to inner strength or maturity. In the New Testament peace is a gift from God to those who are justified by faith (Romans 5:1). The Bible also anticipates peace (absence of conflict and a state of harmonious relations) as being the normal state of affairs among Christians (Mark 9:50). Moreover, Jesus Christ is the Prince of Peace, and His people ought to reflect His image. Lastly, peace was often used as an early Christian greeting when it was linked with grace (Ephesians 1:3).
   b. Answers will vary.
   c. Answers will vary. No one can experience true peace until he or she knows the God of peace. The Bible says those without Christ are

without hope and strangers to the covenants of promise (Ephesians 2:12), which is hardly a state of peace. A non-believer may experience some "circumstantial peace" if peace is defined as the absence of external conflict, but this type of peace is temporal and inferior to that which can be experienced by those who are redeemed and are walking in the Spirit (Galatians 5:22). The believer, by the grace of God, can arrive at a place of spiritual maturity where he or she lives in peace regardless of the external circumstances (Job 13:15; Acts 16:20–25; Philippians 1:19–26).

4. In Ephesians 1:3 the term *heavenlies* refers to the unseen, spiritual dimension or realm where Christ rules supremely and the storehouse from which God's benevolent gifts are given freely to believers based upon their relationship to Christ. In the four additional passages where the phrase occurs in Ephesians (1:20; 2:6; 3:10; 6:12) the scene is more local, as it is in another of Paul's epistles (2 Timothy 4:18). The meaning is that the spiritual blessings of God (the riches of Christ) are found only in heaven and are available to all believers through Christ's sacrifice.

5. a. In the larger context of the New Testament, the spiritual blessings refer to all that is made available to the believer because of Jesus Christ's death and sacrifice. In the immediate context, the phrase refers to the specific spiritual blessings mentioned (adoption, acceptance, redemption, forgiveness, wisdom, inheritance, sealing).
   b. 1. By faith the believer realizes these spiritual blessings are authentic and eternal (2 Corinthians 4:18).
      2. The Christian must believe what God has promised him and claim his inheritance by faith (John 6:29).
      3. The Christian must exercise faith to believe God and His promises (Hebrews 11:1).

6. 1. God chose them so that they would live holy and blameless lives (Ephesians 1:4).
   2. God chose them that they would live their lives filled with praise to Him for all He did on their behalf (Ephesians 1:6, 12).

7. Answers will vary. The question of the exact nature (divine election/human response; limited atonement versus a legitimate offer of salvation to all

men, the security of the believer, etc.) of man's redemption has been the subject of intense theological debate throughout church history. Below is a summary of some of the main perspectives and a few observations/considerations.

1. **Salvation from God's perspective.** All three members of the Godhead are involved in man's redemption. From the Father's perspective, man's redemption was accomplished in eternity past when God the Father chose him for salvation (Ephesians 1:3–4; Acts 2:23). From the perspective of Jesus Christ, man's redemption was accomplished when He died on the cross (John 19:30; Romans 5:8; Ephesians 1:7). From the perspective of the Holy Spirit, redemption is accomplished when man believes the gospel and receives the indwelling Holy Spirit as a pledge or guarantee of his (spiritual) inheritance (Ephesians 1:13–14).
2. **The efficacy of Christ's sacrifice (Who can be saved?).** There are three general views. (1) *The Universalist View*: Proponents of this view teach that since Jesus Christ died for all, all will be eventually saved. This view denies the need for personal repentance toward God and faith in Jesus Christ (Acts 17:30). (2) *The Limited Atonement View*: Jesus Christ died for the elect and the rest will be eternally lost. (3) *The Sufficient-Efficient View*: Jesus Christ died for all (sufficiency; 1 John 2:2), but only those who trust in Him will be saved (John 3:16; Romans 10:13). In this view, Christ's death on the cross was sufficient to redeem all men (Titus 2:11–12), but it's efficient or effective for only those who are saved (John 1:12).
3. **By grace alone.** Man, in his natural state, is spiritually dead in trespasses and sins (Ephesians 2:1). Therefore God must extend grace to quicken him and bring about regeneration. God extends *common grace* to all men (Matthew 5:45; Acts 17:25). He extends *condemning grace* to all men in the form of general revelation (Romans 1:18–20). He extends *convicting grace* to all men (John 16:8–11). He extends *converting* (saving) *grace* to those who believe the gospel and are chosen for salvation (Ephesians 2:8–9).

   Theologian Charles Ryrie (Ryrie Study Bible, note on Ephesians 1:3) provides a concise interpretation of Ephesians 1:3–14 and God's plan of redemption when he says, "God has determined beforehand that those who believe in Christ will be adopted into His family and conformed to His Son (Romans 8:29). It involves a choice on His part

(v. 4); it is done in love (v. 4); it is based on the good pleasure of His will (vv. 5, 9, 11); its purpose is to glorify God (v. 14); but it does not relieve man of his responsibility to believe the gospel in order to bring to pass personally God's predestination (v. 13)."

Theologian J. I. Packer addressed the interrelatedness of divine election and the human responsibility to believe in Jesus Christ alone for eternal life in his helpful book *Evangelism and the Sovereignty of God.* Packer believes the question of divine election and human responsibility remains an antinomy. He describes an "antinomy" as two apparent conflictual laws that address the same subject, but it is unknown how they can be totally reconciled with each other. For example, light can be explained as particles and as waves. What is not clear to scientists is how light can be both waves and particles. Packer goes on to say that the question of divine election and man's responsibility to choose Christ are both taught in Scripture, but their precise interrelatedness remains a mystery.

8. 1. Roman adoption is a picture of God's grace because it was the decision of the father, not the choice or good works of the child.
   2. Roman adoption was irreversible, which is a picture of the believer's security in Christ.
   3. Roman adoption included an irrevocable inheritance to the child, which is a picture of the inheritance believers receive in Christ **(the riches of Christ).**

9. 1. The believer's redemption is **in Him** (Christ). There is salvation in no one other than Christ (Acts 4:12).
   2. The believer's redemption is settled and secure: **we have redemption.**
   3. The believer's redemption was paid for by Christ's death on the cross (**through His blood**). This may seem obvious to most students, but some teach that Christ's sacrifice on the cross, including the shedding of His blood, is not essential for man's salvation. They believe the way Christ lived (His example) is enough to save someone who believes in Christ (the moral ethic argument). The Christian, however, is saved "through His blood" (His sacrifice on the cross), not by His sinless life and example.
   4. The believer's redemption results in the forgiveness of all sins, past, present, and future. There is no time qualification on the sins that are

forgiven. Some teach that Christ paid for the believer's past sins, but he must confess his present sins or lose his salvation. Salvation, as it is stated in Ephesians 1:7, results in the forgiveness of sins—all sins.

10. Answers will vary, but should read something like the following: God's master plan, hidden in ages past but now revealed in Jesus Christ, is to bring all things in heaven and earth under the sovereign authority of Jesus Christ. This grand plan includes those who are saved as well as those who reject Christ. The lost will ultimately acknowledge Christ's sovereign authority in eternal judgment. God's master plan also extends to all creation. When God's master plan is finally fulfilled, all creation will be restored to its original glory and purpose.

11. Individuals must believe the good news (gospel, the word of truth) (Ephesians 1:13). God gives believers the presence (sealing) of the Holy Spirit in their lives.

12. Answers will vary.

Lesson 2: Claiming Your Inheritance

1. a. Paul felt constrained to pray that the Ephesian believers would comprehend the full extent of their spiritual inheritance in Christ (the riches of Christ).
   b. Answers will vary.

2. 1. Even though Christians have been given God's promises, there is a danger of missing them (coming short) (Hebrews 4:1).
   2. The word of God will not profit Christians if they do not accept it by faith (Hebrews 4:2). This happened to the Israelites during the Exodus, and it can happen to believers today.

3. a. Paul prayed that God would give the Ephesians spiritual wisdom and insight (revelation) so that they would know Him more fully.
   b. Paul asked God specifically to give the Ephesian Christians spiritual enlightenment.
   c. Answers will vary.

4. a. John 3:19–20: The unsaved don't expose themselves to the truth because they don't want their deeds (actions) to be revealed.
   b. 1 Corinthians 2:14: The natural (unsaved) person cannot comprehend the things of the Spirit of God. Such people do not possess the Holy Spirit, so the things of God appear foolish to them.
   c. 2 Corinthians 4:3–4: The gospel is veiled (obscured, shrouded) to the unsaved because Satan, who is the god of this world, has blinded their minds.

5. a. Mark 4:13–15: Satan steals the seed of the word of God that is sown in their hearts.
   b. Mark 4:16–17: Some are not committed to the truth, so they fall away from God into error when troubles come into their lives.
   c. Mark 4:18–19: Some people experience spiritual blindness because they are lured away from God by the temptation (deceitfulness) of riches.
   d. Hebrews 5:12–14: Some believers are not diligent about their spiritual growth. If this happens, they can regress spiritually and forget spiritual truths they previously believed.

6. Paul asked God to give the Ephesian believers a clearer vision or understanding of the spiritual reality of their spiritual inheritance in Christ. Paul didn't want them to miss all that God made available to them through Christ's sacrifice. This included much more than merely knowing where they would spend eternity.

7. 1. He asked God to give them assurance of their individual relationship with Him (Ephesians 1:18).
   2. He asked God to give them a better understanding of the true riches of their spiritual inheritance in Christ (Ephesians 1:18).
   3. He asked God to give them a greater understanding of the Holy Spirit's power that raised Jesus Christ from the grave and to help them understand that the same power was available to them (Ephesians 1:19).

8. a. Paul asked God to give the Ephesian Christians absolute assurance and confidence of their eternal relationship with Him. It is only when the Christian has complete assurance of his relationship with God that

he can truly live by faith.
   b. Answers will vary.

9. 1. Jesus has been raised to a place of divine favor because He is now seated at the right hand of the Father (Ephesians 1:20). In Scripture the right hand (of God) figuratively signifies a place of favor (Psalm 110:1).
   2. Jesus has been raised above every other power, on earth and in heaven, from the time of the resurrection through all eternity (Ephesians 1:21).
   3. The resurrection resulted in everything being placed under Christ's authority (Ephesians 1:22).
   4. The resurrection resulted in Jesus being the head of the church (Ephesians 1:22–23).

10. 1. 1 Corinthians 10:13: All believers have been given victory over the temptation to sin. The unsaved person cannot "not sin," but the believer can "not sin." The reality, however, is believers continue to sin because they are not always fully surrendered to Christ in sanctification (1 John 1:8).
   2. 1 Corinthians 15:55–57: Believers also have victory over death because they know they'll be resurrected to newness of life. Christians do not need to fear dying. It's important, however, to distinguish between death and dying. For the believer, death is graduation day, and this thought should bring joy rather than fear. Christians might fear the act of dying, but God can also give them victory over this fearful temptation as well.
   3. Ephesians 2:6: Believers have been given a highly exalted position with Jesus Christ in the heavenlies. This seating with Christ has already taken place.
   4. Colossians 1:13: Believers have been transferred or delivered from the power or domain of darkness into the kingdom of Jesus Christ. Again, this transfer is viewed as having taken place in the past (at the time of salvation), not in the future at the time of physical death.

Lesson 3: Heart of the Problem

1. Answers will vary. The correct answer is man is inherently or innately sinful (Ephesians 2:1–3).

2. In man's natural (unsaved) state, he is spiritually dead in trespasses and sins (Ephesians 2:1). He lives according to the course or pattern of this world instead of God's plan for his life (Ephesians 2:2). Man is directed by Satan (prince of the power of the air), and he is a son or child of disobedience (Ephesians 2:2).

3. 1. We conducted ourselves in the lusts of our flesh.
   2. We fulfilled the desires of the flesh and of the mind.
   3. We were by nature children of wrath just like everyone else. This is the spiritual state of all men before they are saved. Notice Paul includes himself when he says **we all once conducted ourselves** (Ephesians 2:3). All humans follow their own lusts and are being led by the sinful desires of the flesh and the mind (Ephesians 2:3). Man's nature makes him a child under the judgment of God's wrath (Ephesians 2:3).

4. a. Every man has gone astray (spiritually) like a sheep (Isaiah 53:6). Every man is like a spiritually unclean thing, and his righteousness is like filthy rags (Isaiah 64:6).
   b. Man's heart is more deceitful than anything else, and it is desperately wicked (Jeremiah 17:9).
   c. Jesus said man's nature was evil (Matthew 7:11).
   d. Answers will vary, but could include murder, theft, anger, gossip, slander, sexual sin (lust, fornication, adultery, homosexuality, rape, etc.), hatred, greed, and many others.

5. Man sins because he is sinner. The Bible teaches that man is sinful by nature (Ephesians 2:3).

6. a. 1. God is rich in mercy.
      2. God is filled with great love.
   b. God extends His love and grace to man while he is a sinner (Ephesians 2:5).
   c. The timing of man's salvation (when we were dead in trespasses; Ephesians 2:5) proves that man's redemption is entirely a gift of God's grace and not a result of man's good works.

7. a. 1. Ephesians 2:6: At salvation all believers are positionally seated in the heavenlies with Jesus Christ.

2. 2 Corinthians 5:18: At salvation all believers are given a new calling as ambassadors for Christ.
3. Philippians 3:20: At salvation all believers become citizens of heaven.
4. 2 Corinthians 5:20: At salvation all believers receive a divine commission to help reconcile the world to Christ. They become ambassadors for Christ because their citizenship is in heaven.

b. 1. Salvation is by grace (Ephesians 2:8).
   2. Salvation is both certain (**you have been saved**) and present. Ephesians 2:8 says you have been saved, not "you will be saved"—even though that is also true.
   3. Salvation is by grace alone through faith alone. There is nothing else that is necessary for man's salvation.
   4. Salvation is a gift from God. It cannot be earned or purchased.

8. The good works that God has prepared beforehand for the believer to do are likely those that are accomplished entirely for the glory of God by the power of the Holy Spirit.

9. a. When the believer realizes that it is God's grace that saved him, it is God's grace that sanctifies him, and it is God's grace that works in him and through him for God's good pleasure, it brings peace into his life. When a believer "performs" for God, even out of gratitude, it may lead to a work-generating mentality—one that leads the Christian to believe he or she should repay God for salvation. While the believer should be profoundly grateful for salvation, God is the One who works in the believer both to will (motivation) and to do (empowerment) **of His good pleasure** (Philippians 2:13 King James Version).
   b. Answers will vary.

Lesson 4: Temple of God

1. a. Gentile (non-Jewish) believers (Ephesians 2:11–13).
   b. Uncircumcision (Ephesians 2:11).

2. a. 1. They were without Christ.
      2. They were alienated from the Israelite community.

3. They were strangers to the promises or covenants that God gave to the Jews.
4. They had no (eternal) hope in their relationship to God.
5. They were without God in this world.

b. Yes. Before a person is saved or born again, he or she is dead in trespasses and sins (Ephesians 2:1). The individual lives according to Satan's plan instead of God's will, is driven by the lusts of their flesh and minds, and by nature, they are children under (God's) wrath (Ephesians 2:2–3).

c. Unsaved people have no hope or assurance of where they will spend eternity. They also struggle throughout their lives to find hope and meaning in life in a general sense.

3. They must be in Christ, which means they must be redeemed, saved, or born again.

4. Peace. Christ's sacrifice on the cross brought salvation from eternal punishment and with it peace. Peace with God replaces the wrath of God that abides upon the individual before he or she was saved. In Romans 5:1, the word peace doesn't mean peace of mind but rather God's judicial pronouncement of the removal of His wrath toward those who are redeemed.

5. Jesus' death on the cross broke down the wall of separation that divided the two ethnicities and made one new humanity.

6. While it is tempting to see the reference to the middle wall of separation as spiritual inference from the Jerusalem temple where the Jews and the Gentiles were separated, the middle wall is likely a reference to the Mosaic Law that separated Jews and Gentiles because of its regulations and restrictions. The Jews were a people whom God separated to Himself, and the Mosaic Law gave explicit instructions regarding how to maintain this separation. The breaking down of the wall (abolition of the Law or Old Covenant [2 Corinthians 3:7–11]) brought believing Jews and Gentiles into one new body without eliminating their national identities. It is important to note that this new man is NOT the Gentiles becoming Jews.

7. (see chart below)

Non-Christians are ...	Believers are/have ...
Dead in trespasses and sins (vv. 1, 5)	(v. 5) Alive together with Christ
Not saved by their works (v. 9)	(v. 8) Saved by grace through faith
Aliens and strangers to God and His promises (v. 12)	(v. 19) Fellow citizens, members of the household of God
Have no hope (v. 12)	(vs. 14, 16) Christ is our peace, reconciled
Without (access to) God in this world (v. 12)	(v. 18) Through Him (Christ) we both have access to the Father
Far off (from God) (v. 13)	(v. 19) No longer strangers and foreigners

8. 1. Ephesians 2:19: Members of the household of God.
   2. Ephesians 2:21: A holy temple of God.
   3. Ephesians 2:22: Dwelling place of God.
   4. Ephesians 3:21: The church.

9. a. Jesus Christ (Ephesians 2:20).
   b. The apostles and prophets (Ephesians 2:20).
   c. Building stones (individual believers) (1 Peter 2:4).

10. God is pleased when He adds individual believers into His body (1 Corinthians 12:13). God carefully fits each new believer (stones in the analogy; Ephesians 2:21) into His glorious new temple. This new temple is the dwelling place of God in the person of the Holy Spirit (Ephesians 2:22). Believers are the "living stones" who form His spiritual house and serve together as a holy priesthood (1 Peter 2:5). They offer spiritual sacrifices through Jesus Christ to God the Father. This is a glorious picture of the

church of Jesus Christ—one that should cause all believers to glorify God, both personally as they live godly lives, and corporately as they gather together for public worship.

11. Answers will vary.

Lesson 5: A Great Mystery Revealed

1. Paul wanted to explain how he originally learned about this great mystery that Jews and Gentiles were to become fellow citizen and members in God's household. This truth may not seem so earth-shattering after more than 2,000 years, but the thought of believing Jews and Gentiles joined together in one body would have been scandalous at the time—so scandalous that only a revelation from God (a **mystery ... revealed**) would validate this new union.

2. a. The mystery was revealed by revelation from God (Ephesians 3:3) by means of the Holy Spirit. It was revealed to the New Testament apostles and prophets, including Paul (Ephesians 3:5).
   b. 1. He said he had fought the good fight (of faith).
      2. He said he had finished the race, which meant he had been faithful to God and obedient to His will throughout his life.
      3. He said he had kept the faith, which meant he hadn't compromised the truth as a minister of the gospel.

3. Answers will vary.

4. The mystery is not that the Gentiles would be saved, for that was revealed in several Old Testament passages (Isaiah 11:10–11; 42:6; 60:1–3; Amos 9:12; Malachi 1:11). Within the immediate context (Ephesians 2:11–3:21), the mystery hidden in ages past was that Gentile believers, by virtue of their relationship to Jesus Christ, were given equal status with their Hebrew brothers and sisters within the church. Moreover, the Gentile believers could expect full integration into the family of God, and they (we all) share equally in His promises.

5. Answers will vary, but the correct answer is no. Nowhere in Scripture does the Bible state that God's original promises to the nation of Israel have

been voided. On the contrary, the Bible emphasizes that God's promises to Israel are irrevocable (Romans 11:29), and the Bible says He (God) cannot lie (Titus 1:2).

6. 1. God cannot deny Himself (2 Timothy 2:13). God will not deny who He is or His Word.
   2. God cannot change (Hebrews 13:8). Theologians refer to this as His immutability.
   3. God cannot tempt man with evil (James 1:13). When a believer is being tempted to sin, he or she can be certain that the temptation is not coming from God.
   4. God Himself cannot be tempted (James 1:13).

7. Answers will vary.

8. God's master plan, hidden in the past but revealed to the holy apostles and prophets during the early New Testament period, is to manifest or reveal His wisdom to all creation. God did this by allowing Jesus Christ to be the sin sacrifice for both Jews and Gentiles and brought them into a new body, the church, as equal members. The grand demonstration of God's wisdom is now revealed to lost humanity and the entire angelic and demonic worlds (principalities and powers in the heavenlies).

9. a. Answers will vary, but could include the following: The church should focus on honoring God, embracing His calling to manifest His glory to a lost world instead of simply "doing church" or pandering to the people. God's Word reveals the glory of the church, and the church should fully embrace His calling and commission to be His transcendent organism that has been given the unique privilege of revealing His glory and wisdom to this world and the heavenlies. This high calling should be reflected in the mission of the church, the public and private preaching and teaching of the Word, and every aspect of personal and corporate life.
   b. Answers will vary.
   c. Paul was overwhelmed with praise and adoration to God and prayed the Ephesian believers would comprehend the riches of God's glory and understand the love of God that would accomplish this for man.

10. 1. Paul prayed that the Ephesians would be (spiritually) strengthened by means of the Holy Spirit in their inner man (Ephesians 3:16).
    2. He prayed that they would become mature in Christ and trust Him fully (for Christ to dwell in their hearts through faith; Ephesians 3:17).
    3. He prayed that they would develop true spiritual intimacy with Christ and they would be able to comprehend the full extent of God's love for them (Ephesians 3:18–19).
    4. He prayed that they would experience all that God made available to them through Jesus Christ (Ephesians 3:19).

11. 1. God can do more than what we ask Him for or what we can think (Ephesians 3:20).
    2. God can perform more than we can ask or think by the (Holy Spirit) power that lives within us and works through us.
    3. The Bible says all glory (credit, praise, adoration, worth) belongs to God in Jesus Christ. This glory should be directed toward God forever by all people.

Lesson 6: Worthy of God's Calling

1. a. For the believer to walk (live) worthy of God's calling on his life, he must personally embrace God's master plan, live a holy life as a living sacrifice, glory in his spiritual inheritance (the riches of Christ), and seek to be an active participant in the building of His glorious temple. Only then can a Christian say that he has fully embraced his high calling in Christ and is walking worthy of the Lord.
   b. It is likely that Paul, under the inspiration of the Holy Spirit, wrote these words to help the Ephesians believers understand the full extent of Christ's authority over their lives. Perhaps Paul also referred to himself as a prisoner to keep the Ephesian believers from become prideful of their high calling in Christ. They were to realize that they were servants of God, and this calling might lead them into personal suffering as faithful followers of Jesus Christ.

2. a. Believers should adopt true Christlike humility (lowliness). This is not a man-centered, self-effacing, self-deprecating demeanor but rather a deliberate, continuous submission to the person and will of God. This Christlike humility should manifest itself in true gentleness of manner

and speech and patience (longsuffering) toward others. Believers should be willing to make allowances for the failures (not deliberate sins) of others.

b. 1. They lie to one another (Ephesians 4:25).
   2. They also allow ungodly speech to proceed from their mouths (Ephesians 4:29).
   3. They also allow bitterness or resentment, anger, shouting, and evil speaking to proceed out of their mouths (Ephesians 4:31).
   4. They slander other people (Proverbs 10:18).

3.

One body	the church (the body of Christ).
One Spirit	the Holy Spirit
One hope	the assurance of eternal life in Christ or the hope believers have in Christ's return and being united with Him.
One Lord	Jesus Christ.
One faith	the revelation or truth that was given by Jesus Christ through the apostles and prophets and is now revealed to us in God's Word (Jude 3).
One baptism	Spirit baptism that places every new believer into the body of Christ (1 Corinthians 12:13; Titus 3:5).

4. Answers will vary but should reflect something like the following. The believer must realize his ultimate loyalty is to Jesus Christ, not a church or a denomination. Believers must also realize that they are in a spiritual war and are called to be defenders of the truth, not only against a world that doesn't know God, but against spiritual compromise within the church. The Bible is replete with warnings against spiritual compromise and laden with admonitions to hold fast to the truth (Galatians 1:6–10; Philippians 2:16; Colossians 2:4–23; 1 Timothy 1:3–6; 2 Timothy 4:1–4; Titus 1:5–9; 2 Peter 2; Jude 3). The believer, however, must remember to always stand for the truth in a spirit of love (Ephesians 4:15).

5. a. The spiritual gifts are given to the church to equip believers so they can do the work of Christ's ministry. This includes building up the body

of Christ and reaching the unsaved with the message of salvation.

b. It is God who gives all spiritual enlightenment or growth (1 Corinthians 3:5–7, Hebrews 12:3). God calls specific believers and gives them spiritual gifts so they can serve Him and equip (not just teach) His church (Ephesians 4:12). The entire church is to do the work of the ministry, which includes building up the body of Christ by means of holy living, encouraging and edifying other believers, and making disciples (Matthew 28:18–20).

6. This calling continues until every believer becomes mature in Christ and they become all Christ intended them to be (Ephesians 4:13–14).

7. 1. A primary indicator of spiritual immaturity is a lack of spiritual discernment which causes the believer to be susceptible to false teachers and false doctrine (Ephesians 4:14). Paul admonishes his readers and exhorts them to grow up in Christ. He said all believers should get past the stage of spiritual infancy.
   2. A second indication that a believer has not reached spiritual maturity is that he or she is still in the learning stage and not ministering God's Word to others (Hebrews 5:11–12). While believers should always be growing in their relationship with God, they ought to reach a level of spiritual growth where they are able to instruct others about God's truth.

8. a. Jesus invited certain of His followers to walk (live) with Him as He ministered to others (Mark 1:17). He said, **Follow Me, and I will make you become fishers of men.** Christ's approach to **equipping ... the saints for the work of ministry** (Ephesians 4:12) should not be overlooked. He trained the disciples rather than simply teaching them the principles of fulfilling the Great Commission. In fact, Jesus reiterates his commitment to training His disciples for the work of the ministry in Matthew 28:20 when He says **teaching them <u>to observe</u> all things**. Believers need to be taught God's Word, but true discipleship (equipping the saints for their work in ministry) goes beyond teaching to include training.

   b. The modern understanding of teaching includes two things: (1) Effective communication of specific information by a teacher to a student, and (2) an appropriate evaluation of the student's ability to comprehend the specific information that was taught. Training incorporates these two aspects of teaching, but adds a commitment on behalf of the teacher to ensure that the student becomes fully trained (**teaching them to observe all things that I have commanded you**; Matthew 28:20). Jesus made this distinction clear when He said, **It is enough for a disciple that he be <u>like</u> his teacher** (Matthew 10:25; NASB: "become like his teacher"). Jesus did not say that it was enough for a disciple to know as much as his teacher. This same concept is also clear in the book of Proverbs where Solomon says, **I have not <u>obeyed</u> the voice of my teachers** (Proverbs 5:13).

9. 1. Believers will be united in the faith (Ephesians 4:13).
   2. Believers will become spiritually mature (**come to the unity ... of the knowledge of the Son of God, to a perfect** [spiritually mature] **man** [believer]) (Ephesians 4:13).
   3. Believers will develop spiritual discernment (**no longer ... tossed ... and carried about**; Ephesians 4:14).
   4. Believers will learn how to communicate spiritual truth in a spirit of love (Ephesians 4:15). They will be neither ear-tickling compromisers who forsake the truth nor crude dispensers of truth who have little regard for the Lord's command to love others.
   5. Believers will grow into Christ, their head (Ephesians 4:15).
   6. Believers will embrace their God-given spiritual responsibility of building up the body of Christ (Ephesians 4:16).
   7. Believers will be knit together because every believer is fulfilling his or her role within the body of Christ (Ephesians 4:16).
   8. The body of Christ will grow (personally in faith and numerically in size) (Ephesians 4:16).

Lesson 7: The New Man

1. a. This means to stop living like an unsaved individual.
   b. 1. Their understanding is darkened (Ephesians 4:18). The J B Phillips version of the New Testament says, "they live blindfold in a world of illusion."
      2. They are alienated from the life of God (Ephesians 4:18).
      3. They are ignorant of God and His ways (Ephesians 4:18).

4. Their hearts (minds, emotions) are blinded to the reality of God (Ephesians 4:18; 2 Corinthians 4:4).
5. Their conscience, which is a gift from God, has become seared and no longer serves as an effective moral compass for them (Ephesians 4:19).
6. They have given themselves to sensuality (lewdness) and other forms of unholy conduct, including greed (Ephesians 4:19).

2. The believer must learn Christ, not just about Him. This means much more than learning a few things or even many things about the person of Jesus Christ. It means developing an intimate, spiritual relationship with Jesus Christ through God's Word (personal Bible study, meditation, confession of sin, Scripture memory, and faithfully listening to the preaching of God's Word in a church where the Word of God is honored) and learning to walk in the Spirit.

3. a. God commands believers to take personal responsibility for putting off the old man or self—the way of the Gentiles (unsaved). This includes forsaking every thought, action, and habit that is contrary to new life in Christ (2 Corinthians 10:4–5) and learning to walk in the Spirit (Galatians 5:16–18). The believer must surrender his thoughts to God and bring every thought under the authority of Jesus Christ (2 Corinthians 10:4–5). This means that whenever a believer's thoughts contradict what the Bible says, he should reject his thoughts and accept what God's Word says. To do this, the believer must know the mind of Christ and learn to walk in the Spirit (Galatians 5:16–18). The believer must fully surrender himself moment by moment to the will of God and be sensitive to the Holy Spirit's leading.
   b. Answers will vary.
   c. No. Even though a Christian is diligent about "putting off" the old sin nature, the sinful nature of man is not eradicated and the believer must still deal with its influence in his life. The "putting off" of the sinful nature refers to not allowing it to be an active voice in the believer's life. The Christian, saved by grace and sanctified by God's Word and the Holy Spirit, is empowered to walk in a new life—the life of Christ. While the old sinful nature will continue to tempt him, he does not need to succumb to its invitations and solicitations to sin.

4. a. Matthew responded immediately by leaving his old life and following Jesus (Matthew 9:9).
   b. Jesus told the woman to sin no more (John 8:11). Jesus didn't tell her to enroll in a sex addiction class or to get years of therapy. He told her to "stop it." While Jesus' advice may seem simplistic, He calls individuals to obedience and promises to give them the power to obey. A Christian can trust Him and rely on the Holy Spirit's power to resist temptation and believe that God will not give him more than he can bear (1 Corinthians 10:13; James 4:7–8).
   c. Answers will vary.

5. a. Ephesians 4:25:
      1. Don't lie.
      2. Speak truth.
      3. Because we are related to (members) one another in Christ.
   b. Ephesians 4:26–27:
      1. Be angry. This is not an imperative, but rather a recognition that anger can be triggered by our own sinful desires (James 4:1–3) or the sin of others (righteous anger or indignation; cf. Hebrews 3:12–17).
      2. Don't let the sun go down on your wrath (yield all angry feelings to God each day).
      3. If you don't deal with your anger, you will be giving the devil an opportunity or foothold to work in your life for your destruction.
   c. Ephesians 4:28:
      1. Don't steal.
      2. Work.
      3. So you can give to others in need.
   d. Ephesians 4:29:
      1. Don't speak corrupt speech.
      2. Speak things that build others up.
      3. So that your speech may give grace to the hearers.

6. In Ephesians 4:30 the first word ("and") links the prohibition against grieving the Holy Spirit with the admonitions in the preceding verses. The reader, therefore, should not understand God's prohibition to refrain from grieving the Holy Spirit as some abstract command but realize it is intricately linked to God's commands in the preceding verses. The Holy

Spirit is grieved anytime believers dismiss God's commands, treating them as options rather than imperatives to be fulfilled by the power of the Spirit. But grieving the Holy Spirit includes more than the immediate commands and prohibitions in the preceding passage. It includes "putting off" all that Christ commanded His followers to forsake and "putting on" all that God commands His followers to practice.

7. Bitterness, wrath (NIV: "rage"), anger, clamor (NIV: "brawling"), evil speaking (NIV: "slander"), malice.

8. Christians must understand that any sin a person committed against them pales in comparison to their own sin against God. Since Jesus Christ forgives believers entirely and completely and does not hold their sin against them, believers ought to forgive those who have sinned against them in the same manner (entirely and completely).

9. Answers will vary.

Lesson 8: Imitators of God

1. a. To be an imitator of God means more than mechanically mimicking Christ's manner of speaking and actions. Since Christianity is the religion of the heart, a Christian can only truly imitate God when he seeks to yield his life to Him in every area.
   b. Answers will vary.

2. a. 1. Jesus loved man (Ephesians 5:2).
      2. Jesus gave His life for man (Ephesians 5:2).
      3. Jesus always did what pleased the Father (John 8:29).
      4. Jesus glorified the Father while He was on earth and finished the work that God gave Him to do (John 17:4).
      5. Jesus declared God's love to man (John 17:26)
   b. As an offering and a sacrifice, which was a sweet-smelling aroma to the father.
   c. The fragrance or aroma of Jesus Christ (2 Corinthians 2:15).

3. 1. Fornication (Ephesians 5:3).
   2. Uncleanness (Ephesians 5:3).

3. Covetousness. (Ephesians 5:3).
4. Filthiness (Ephesians 5:4).
5. Foolish talking (Ephesians 5:4).
6. Coarse jesting (Ephesians 5:4).

4. The believer should not judge the unsaved for their behavior, either outwardly or in his heart for two reasons: (1) God commands believers not to judge them (1 Corinthians 5:9–13), and (2) nonbelievers aren't able to honor God and obey His commands because they are not indwelt with the Spirit of God. If a Christian understands this, it will likely keep him from acting "holier than thou." Also, the believer should always realize that he was saved by grace and not by his own good works. This should lead to a profound sense of humility. Finally, if a believer learns to deal with sin in his own life before he is tempted to judge another person, he will be humbled before God, which will keep him from coming across as "holier than thou" to others. On the other hand, it's important to realize that a believer cannot stop another person from judging him for his stand for Christ. He must never compromise the truth just because another person might accuse him of being "holier than thou."

5. a. 1. Both are selfish and self-centered.
   2. Both focus on personal gratification rather than on doing God's will.
   3. Both eventually produce emptiness and remorse.
   4. Other answers could apply.

   b. All manner of sexual impurity that is not specifically identified in the passage.

6. Those who persist in living in sexual sin will have no inheritance in the kingdom of Christ and God (Ephesians 5:5). They will perish in the lake of fire (Revelation 21:8).

7. a. Answers will vary, but could include the following: "Living together or being sexually active is not wrong if we love each other." "It's not sex as long as we don't engage in sexual intercourse." "God can't expect me to be celibate when He hasn't brought me a spouse." "God doesn't really care about personal things like somebody's sex life." "Nobody has the right to tell me what I can or can't do with my own body."

"You shouldn't be judging others about their private lives. Nobody has the right to do that." "We are planning to get married. It is just more convenient to live together so we can save money."

b. Answers will vary.

8. All believers lived in spiritual darkness before they were saved, but they are brought into the light (of God) through salvation in Jesus Christ (Ephesians 5:8). They are indwelt with the Spirit of God, and the fruit of the Spirit within them should be goodness, righteousness, and truth (Ephesians 5:9).

9. a. The command in Ephesians 5:11–12 is in relation to fellow members of the body of Christ. As fellow members of God's family, believers should accept their family responsibility to watch over one another in love. They should allow God's love and a love for their fellow believers to cover (overlook) many of their faults and failings, realizing all believers are in a process of spiritual development (John 14:21). However, if they see another Christian sinning in a way that harms the testimony of Christ or causes spiritual harm to others, the (non-sinning) believer should examine his own life and then lovingly confront the sinning believer (Galatians 6:1).

   b. 1. Christians should let God's wisdom guide all areas of their lives. They should be alert to things around them (**walk circumspectly**), be watchful for opportunities to glorify God, and avoid sin and temptation (Ephesians 5:15).

      2. Christians should make the best use of the time that God gives them. They should value God's gift of life and not squander any opportunities to serve Him (Ephesians 5:16).

      3. Christians should seek to understand God's will for their lives. To do this they should search the Scriptures daily, attend a good Bible-believing church, and pray earnestly for God's leading in their lives on a moment-by-moment basis (Ephesians 5:17).

10. a. To be filled with the Holy Spirit means to be controlled by or under the influence of the Holy Spirit. In the same way as a drunk person's thoughts, speech, and actions are controlled by the alcohol, a believer should allow his thoughts, speech, and actions to be controlled by the Spirit.

    b. 1. A Christian who is filled with the Spirit will overflow with praise to

God in the presence of other people (Ephesians 5:19).
2. A Christian who is filled with the Spirit will continually express profound gratitude to God for all that He allows to come into His life (Ephesians 5:20).
3. A Christian who is filled with the Spirit will be willing to submit to others because he desires to honor the Lord and reflect Christlike humility in his relationship with others. The word "entreatable" or the phrase "sweetness of disposition" could also be used to describe this Holy Spirit–generated quality (Ephesians 5:21).

11. Answers will vary.

Lesson 9: Spirit-Filled Living

1. a. A Christian woman demonstrates that she is filled with the Spirit when she yields herself to her husband's God-appointed leadership (Ephesians 5:22). The word "submitting" is the fifth of a string of participles (think "ing" words) in Ephesians 5:19–22—all describing what it means to be filled with the Spirit. Second, a Christian woman demonstrates that she is filled with the Spirit when she respects her husband (Ephesians 5:33).
   b. A Christian husband demonstrates that he is filled with Spirit when he loves his wife as Christ loved the church, loves his wife as he does his own body, and loves his wife as himself (Ephesians 5:25, 28, 33). Moreover, a Christian husband demonstrates that he is filled with the Spirit when he submits to his wife in the fear of the Lord (Ephesians 5:21). This mutual submission of the husband and wife honors each other and the Lord and brings a sweetness to the marriage relationship.
   c. Some men struggle to understand the difference between a true God-defined love and sexual desire for their spouse. By defining what it means for a husband to truly love his wife, as well as repeating it three times in the same passage, this passage helps Christian men understand how to love their wives as Christ commanded.

2. 1. Chauvinism defines a group's prejudicial relationship toward another group. The biblical injunction for a wife to submit to her husband's God-ordained leadership responsibility is individual. The wife is not required to submit to other men.

   2. Chauvinism is humanistic in origin and conflictual by nature. Biblical submission is divine in origin and complementary by nature.
   3. Other answers could apply.

3. a. 1. Christ sacrificed His life for the church (Ephesians 5:25).
      2. Christ ministers to the church with grace and patience. He cleanses and washes the church from the stain of sin through the Word (Ephesians 5:26).
      3. Christ desires the best for the church (that she should be **a glorious church without spot or wrinkle**; Ephesians 5:27).
   b. Answers will vary, but could include the following:
      1. He should seek to extend Christ's love to her each day through the power of the Holy Spirit.
      2. He should value her in the same way Christ values the church.
      3. He should believe in her in the same way Christ believes in His church and wants the best for her.
      4. He should pray over her, lovingly guide her in the Word, live a godly life before her, and wait patiently for Christ to work in her life until she becomes all that God wants her to be.

4. 1. Husbands are to love their wives as their own bodies (Ephesians 5:28).
   2. Husbands are to love their wives as they love themselves (Ephesians 5:28–29).

5. There are two possible interpretations for this command.
   1. While there are some exceptions (self-mutilation, suicide) man loves himself and cares for himself intuitively and naturally cares for his own needs. In the same way a Christian husband is commanded to provide this same care for his wife. It is not something he should have to deliberately and consciously think to do. He should naturally love his wife in this way.
   2. When a man and a woman are joined together in marriage, they become one flesh (Genesis 2:24; Ephesians 5:31). The thought is that the man is to love his wife in such a way that he sees her as part of himself. No longer does he see her as separate (although she still has her own identity), but rather he sees and loves his wife as part of himself. This interpretation may be particularly important to men who have a strong competitive nature and see most things from a competitive perspective.

6. a. Answers will vary.
   b. The Bible exhorts her to win her husband to Christ not by nagging but by allowing Jesus Christ to shine through her life (1 Peter 3:1). She should be respectful toward him and seek to be pure in her thoughts, attitudes, and actions (1 Peter 3:2). She should seek to allow Christ to develop an inner beauty (a gentle and quiet spirit) that is very precious in God's sight (1 Peter 3:4). This means not that she shouldn't take care of her appearance but rather that her focus should be on her relationship with God.

7. 1. Both the man and the woman should establish an adult relationship with their parents. The phrase "leave your father and mother" doesn't mean to move a long distance away. It means that the new marriage results in a new home and a new entity. No longer is the newly married couple under the authority of their parents. This is made clear in many marriage ceremonies when the father of the bride "gives his daughter away."
   2. Marriage is a powerful union between a man and a woman (not a man and a man, a woman and a woman, etc.). God is the architect of marriage, and everyone entering marriage would be wise to follow His plan for a successful marriage.
   3. The marriage of a man and a woman results in their becoming "one flesh." This phrase not only speaks about their sexual union; it speaks to the depth and permanence of the marriage bond from God's perspective.

8. The word *mystery*, as we learned earlier in this study, is not something unknowable. It is something that was unknown in the past and now has been made known through God's revelation to man. What is this mystery about marriage that God has now revealed? Specifically, when a husband loves his wife as Christ loves the church and the wife respects her husband, this presents a picture of Christ's love for His church.

9. a. Children can obey and honor their parents.
   b. Fathers should bring their children up in the ways of the Lord. Parents should not provoke, exasperate, or overcorrect their children or live hypocritical Christian lives before them. They should instruct them in the ways of the Lord, both by teaching them God's Word and by modeling the Christ-life before them.

10. a. 1. Christian workers should perform their work responsibilities as if they were working directly for Jesus Christ. They should work diligently at all times, not just when they are being watched by their superiors (Ephesians 6:5).
    2. Christian workers should realize that they are doing God's will when they do their work well (Ephesians 6:6–7). Their work is a spiritual sacrifice that is pleasing to God; it is not just a secular job.
    3. Christian workers should realize that God is watching them, and the Lord will repay them for their work (Ephesians 6:8).

    b. Christian employers should lead in a way that honors the Lord. They should not lead by constantly threatening their employees. They should also realize that God has authority over them, and He will hold them accountable for how they lead. The Lord will also judge them if they don't lead according to His will (Ephesians 6:9).

11. a. Answers will vary.
    b. Answers will vary.

Lesson 10: The Great Cosmic Conflict

1. a. 1. A Christian who is strong in the Lord has learned to rely on God's strength rather than his own (Ephesians 6:10). He has learned that his own strength will not sustain him during life's conflicts, and he has learned to rely on the Lord and to trust His Word.
   2. A Christian who is strong in the Lord doesn't allow doubts to control his thinking. He has learned God's Word is true and that he can fully rely on Him. The believer who has come to this point of trust in God doesn't waver in his or her trust in Him during trials (Romans 4:20).
   3. A Christian who is strong in the Lord relies on God's grace to be the source of power and strength to fulfill His will (2 Timothy 2:1).

   b. Answers will vary.

2. a. Christians can only be strong in the Lord when they rely on the (Holy Spirit) power God provides (Ephesians 6:10). They must learn to live by faith (Romans 4:20) and must allow grace to be their strength (2 Timothy 2:1).

b. Believers need assurance that they can withstand the vicious attacks of the devil.

3. The devil or wicked one (Ephesians 6:11, 16), principalities, powers, rulers of the darkness, and spiritual hosts of wickedness (Ephesians 6:12).

4. a. 1. Genesis 2:15–17; 3:1: He introduces doubt in the veracity (truthfulness) of God's word (**Has God indeed said…?**)
   2. Genesis 3:3–4: He denies God's Word (**You will not surely die**).
   3. Genesis 3:5: He causes people to question (doubt) God's motives and appeals to their desire for enlightenment.
   4. 2 Peter 2:1–2: He uses false teachers to secretly introduce false teachings and destructive heresies.

   b. 1. Proverbs 1:10–19: The enemy uses ungodly people who promise a quick and easy reward without negative consequences.
   2. Proverbs 5:1–5: The enemy uses immoral people to entice naïve fools into sexual sin.
   3. Daniel 4:28–33: The enemy convinces some that their own ability is the sole basis of their success.
   4. Mark 7:9–13: The enemy helps some teach man-made religious traditions as truth. This is used to draw believers away from the truth.
   5. I Timothy 6:9: The enemy uses the lure or enticement of financial riches to destroy lives.

   c. The enemy comes to kill, steal, and destroy. The devil's goal is to kill, steal, and destroy. He is the greatest mass murderer (suicide, drug-related deaths, murder, death in the name of false religions, etc.). He is the greatest thief, robbing man of his God-given potential and stealing peace, joy, hope, etc. He is the greatest destroyer of relationships, human potential, etc.

5. 1. Both are close combat.
   2. Both are personal. This is a one-on-one conflict.
   3. Both could be deadly. Ancient wrestling matches could result in death of one of the combatants, and Satan comes to kill (John 10:10).
   4. Both could use deception to gain advantage or subdue an opponent.
   5. Both require constant vigilance to defeat the enemy.

   Other answers could apply.

6. a. The Roman soldier wore a loose tunic over a leather belt or girdle. On his belt he secured the scabbard that held his sword. This reference to truth cannot refer to God's Word because that is represented by the sword of the Spirit (Ephesians 6:17). The reference to truth in Ephesians 6:14 likely refers to the believer's need to be saturated in God's Word so he knows what God wants him to do in the heat of battle. The Christian soldier is protected and guided by truth in the face of temptation.
   b. The breastplate of righteousness is closely linked to the previous phrase. The Christian soldier's conduct should be guided by truth and is also to be guided by righteousness. A believer who stands in truth (integrity) and is committed to righteous conduct regardless of the outcome of the battle will be victorious over his enemies. He or she will look to God for strength and victory and remain righteous in conflict.
   c. There are two possible interpretations. (1) In the face of attack, the believer should always be ready to proclaim the gospel. It is called the gospel of peace because it satisfies God's wrath toward the repentant sinner and brings peace in its place. The believer must be always prepared to advance the cause of Christ even during times of intense spiritual conflict. (2) An ancient soldier's footwear (a hobnailed sandal) was important to his stability in conflict. In the same way, a personal knowledge of the gospel, and its ultimate victory over all spiritual conflict, will strengthen and stabilize a believer during spiritual conflict.
   d. The shield of faith refers to reliance upon God. When believers face a spiritual attack, they quickly realize their resources (personal determination, etc.) are insufficient to overcome the enemy. Wise is the believer who makes the Lord his strength and confidence.
   e. The helmet of salvation refers to the believer's assurance that he has been redeemed and his salvation is by grace. While he might be tempted to think the attack he's facing is God's punishment for some past sin, he can be assured that his salvation has been secured not by his good works but by Christ's sacrifice on his behalf. All his sins have been atoned for, and knowing this will strengthen him greatly in life's battles.
   f. The word of God.

7. Answers will vary but should include something like the following: Believers should be aware of the reality and danger of spiritual warfare, but they

should not allow themselves to take their eyes off Jesus Christ or His authority and power over all things (1 John 4:4). Moreover, they should pray for themselves and other believers as Paul encouraged the Ephesians to do (Ephesians 6:18–19). They should continue to advance the gospel, knowing that the message of salvation and the proclamation of the truth are the best weapons against the advance of the enemy.

8. a. Paul asked the Ephesians to pray that God would give him more boldness to share the gospel. He said he ought to be spreading the Word more, and he needed God's strength to do what he had been commissioned to do.
   b. Answers will vary.

9. a. Answers will vary.
   b. Answers will vary.

10. Answers will vary.

Final Exam

Every person will eventually stand before God in judgment—the final exam. The Bible says, ***And it is appointed for men to die once, but after this the judgment*** (Hebrews 9:27).

May I ask you a question? *If you died today, do you know for certain you would go to heaven?* I did not ask if you're religious or a church member, nor did I ask if you've had some encounter with God—a meaningful spiritual experience. I didn't even ask if you believe in God or angels or if you're trying to live a good life. The question I *am* asking is this: *If you died today, do you know for certain you would go to heaven?*

When you die, you will stand alone before God in judgment. You'll either be saved for all eternity, or you will be separated from God for all eternity in what the Bible calls the lake of fire (Romans 14:12; Revelation 20:11–15). Tragically, many religious people who believe in God are not going to be accepted by Him when they die.

> ***Many will say to Me in that day, "Lord, Lord, have we not prophesied in Your name, cast out demons in Your name, and done many wonders in Your name?" And then I will declare to them, "I never knew you; depart from Me, you who practice lawlessness!"*** (Matthew 7:22–23)

God loves you and wants you to go to heaven (John 3:16; 2 Peter 3:9). If you are not sure where you'll spend eternity, you are not prepared to meet God. God wants you to know for certain that you will go to heaven.

> ***Behold, now is the accepted time; behold, now is the day of salvation.*** (2 Corinthians 6:2)

The words ***behold*** and ***now*** are repeated because God wants you to know that you can be saved today. You do not need to hear those terrible words, ***Depart from Me ....*** Isn't that great news?

Jesus himself said, ***You must be born again*** (John 3:7). These aren't the words of a pastor, a church, or a particular denomination. They're the words of Jesus Christ himself. You *must* be born again (saved from eternal damnation) before you die; otherwise, it will be too late when you die! You can know for certain today that God will accept you into heaven when you die.

These things I have written to you who believe in the name of the Son of God, that you may* know *that you have eternal life.

(1 John 5:13)

The phrase ***you may know*** means that you can know for certain before you die that you will go to heaven. To be born again, you must understand and accept four essential spiritual truths. These truths are right from the Bible, so you know you can trust them—they are not man-made religious traditions. Now, let's consider these four essential spiritual truths.

Essential Spiritual Truth

#1

The Bible teaches that you are a sinner and separated from God.

No one is righteous in God's eyes. To be righteous means to be totally without sin, not even a single act.

There is none righteous, no, not one;
There is none who understands;
There is none who seeks after God.
They have all turned aside;
They have together become unprofitable;
There is none who does good, no, not one.
(Romans 3:10–12)

...for all have sinned and fall short of the glory of God.
(Romans 3:23)

Look at the words God uses to show that all men are sinners—**none, not one, all turned aside, not one**. God is making a point: all of us are sinners. No one is good (perfectly without sin) in His sight. The reason is sin.

Have you ever lied, lusted, hated someone, stolen anything, or taken God's name in vain, even once? These are all sins.

Are you willing to admit to God that you are a sinner? If so, then tell Him right now you have sinned. You can say the words in your heart or aloud—it doesn't matter which—but be honest with God. Now check the box if you have just admitted you are a sinner.

❒ God, I admit I am a sinner in Your eyes.

Now, let's look at the second essential spiritual truth.

Essential Spiritual Truth

#2

The Bible teaches that you cannot save yourself or earn your way to heaven.

Man's sin is a very serious problem in the eyes of God. Your sin separates you from God, both now and for all eternity—unless you are born again.

> ***For the wages of sin is death.***
> (Romans 6:23)

> ***And you He made alive, who were dead in trespasses and sins.***
> (Ephesians 2:1)

Wages are a payment a person earns by what he or she has done. Your sin has earned you the wages of death, which means separation from God. If you die never having been born again, you will be separated from God after death.

You cannot save yourself or purchase your entrance into heaven. The Bible says that man is **not redeemed with corruptible things, like silver or gold** (1 Peter 1:18). If you owned all the money in the world, you still could not buy your entrance into heaven. Neither can you buy your way into heaven with good works.

> ***For by grace you have been saved through faith, and that not of yourselves; it is the gift of God, not of works, lest anyone should boast.*** (Ephesians 2:8–9)

The Bible says salvation is **not of yourselves**. It is **not of works, lest anyone should boast**. Salvation from eternal judgment cannot be earned by doing good works; it is a gift of God. There is nothing you can do to purchase your way into heaven because you are already unrighteous in God's eyes.

If you understand you cannot save yourself, then tell God right now that you are a sinner, separated from Him, and you cannot save yourself. Check the box below if you have just done that.

❒ God, I admit that I am separated from You because of my sin. I realize that I cannot save myself.

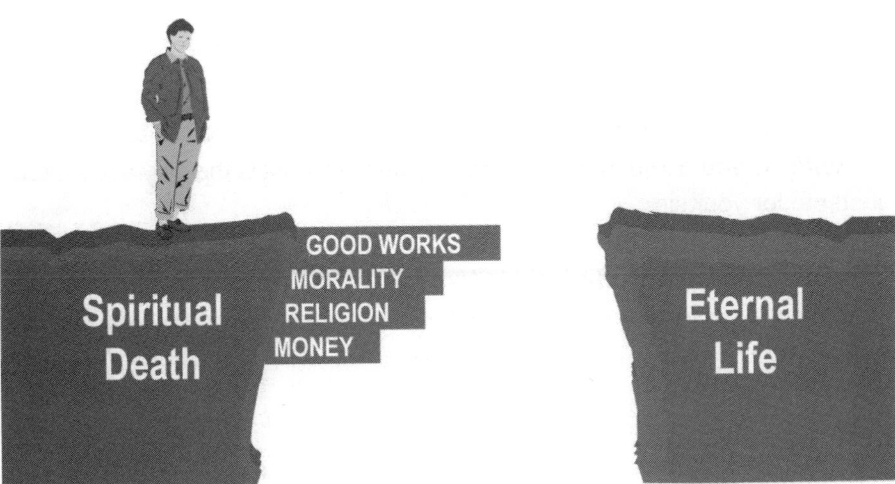

Now, let's look at the third essential spiritual truth.

Essential Spiritual Truth

#3

The Bible teaches that Jesus Christ died on the cross to pay the complete penalty for your sin and to purchase a place in heaven for you.

Jesus Christ, the sinless Son of God, lived a perfect life, died on the cross, and rose from the dead to pay the penalty for your sin and purchase a place in heaven for you. He died on the cross on your behalf, in your place, as your substitute, so you do not have to go to hell. Jesus Christ is the only acceptable substitute for your sin.

> ***For He [God, the Father] made Him [Jesus] who knew [committed] no sin to be sin for us, that we might become the righteousness of God in Him.***
> (2 Corinthians 5:21)

> ***I [Jesus] am the way, the truth, and the life. No one comes to the Father except through Me.***
> (John 14:6)

Nor is there salvation in any other, for there is no other name under heaven given among men by which we must be saved.
(Acts 4:12)

Jesus Christ is your only hope and means of salvation. Because you are a sinner, you cannot pay for your sins, but Jesus paid the penalty for your sins by dying on the cross in your place. Friend, there is salvation in no one else—not angels, not some religious leader, not even your religious good works. No religious act such as baptism, confirmation, or joining a church can save you. There is no other way, no other name that can save you. Only Jesus Christ can save you. You must be saved by accepting Jesus Christ's substitutionary sacrifice for your sins, or you will be lost forever.

Do you see clearly that Jesus Christ is the only way to God in heaven? If you understand this truth, tell God that you understand, and check the box below.

❐ God, I understand that Jesus Christ died to pay the penalty for my sin. I understand that His death on the cross was the only acceptable sacrifice for my sin.

Essential Spiritual Truth

#4

By faith, you must trust in Jesus Christ alone for eternal life and call upon Him to be your Savior and Lord.

Many religious people admit they have sinned. They believe Jesus Christ died for the sins of the world, but they are not saved. Why? Thousands of moral, religious people have never completely placed their faith in Jesus Christ *alone* for eternal life. They think they must believe in Jesus Christ as a real person and do good works to earn their way to heaven. They are not trusting Jesus Christ alone. To be saved, you must trust in Jesus Christ *alone* for eternal life. Look what the Bible teaches about trusting Jesus Christ alone for salvation.

> ***Believe on the Lord Jesus Christ, and you will be saved.***
> (Acts 16:31)

> ***...that if you confess with your mouth the Lord Jesus and* believe *in your heart that God has raised Him from the dead, you will be saved. For with the heart one believes unto righteousness, and with the mouth confession is made unto salvation.... For there is no distinction between Jew and Greek, for the same Lord over all is rich to all who call upon Him. For "whoever calls on the name of the Lord shall be saved.***
> (Romans 10:9–10, 12–13)

Do you see what God is saying? To be saved or born again, you must trust Jesus Christ *alone* for eternal life. Jesus Christ paid for your complete salvation. Jesus said, **It is finished!** (John 19:30). Jesus paid for your salvation completely when He shed His blood on the cross for your sin.

If you believe that God resurrected Jesus Christ (proving God's acceptance of Jesus as a worthy sacrifice for man's sin) and you are willing to confess Jesus Christ as your Savior and Lord (master of your life), you will be saved.

Friend, right now God is offering you the greatest gift in the world. God wants to give you the *gift* of eternal life, the *gift* of His complete forgiveness for all your sins, and the *gift* of His unconditional acceptance into heaven when you die. Will you accept His free gift now, right where you are?

Are you unsure how to receive the gift of eternal life? Let me help you. Do you remember that I said you needed to understand and accept four essential spiritual truths? First, you admitted you are a sinner. Second, you admitted you were separated from God because of your sin and you could not save yourself. Third, you realized that Jesus Christ is the only way to heaven—no other name can save you.

Now, you must trust that Jesus Christ died once and for all to save your lost soul. Just take God at His word—He will not lie to you! This is the kind of simple faith you need to be saved. If you would like to be saved right now, right where you are, offer this prayer of simple faith to God. Remember, the words must come from your heart.

> **God, I am a sinner and deserve to go to hell. Thank You, Jesus, for dying on the cross for me and for purchasing a place in heaven for me. I believe You are the Son of God and You are able to save me right now. Please forgive me for my sin and take me to heaven when I die. I invite You into my life as Savior and Lord, and I trust You alone for eternal life. Thank You for giving me the gift of eternal life. Amen.**

If, in the best way you know how, you trusted Jesus Christ alone to save you, then God just saved you. He said in His Holy Word, ***But as many as received Him, to them He gave the right to become the children of God*** (John 1:12). It's that simple. God just gave you the gift of eternal life by faith. You have just been born again, according to the Bible.

You will not come into eternal judgment, and you will not perish in the lake of fire—you are saved forever! Read this verse carefully and let it sink into your heart.

> ***Most assuredly, I say to you, he who hears My word and believes in Him who sent Me has everlasting life, and shall not come into judgment, but has passed from death into life.***
> (John 5:24)

Now, let me ask you a few more questions.

According to God's holy Word (John 5:24), not your feelings, what kind of life did God just give you? ________________________________

What two words did God say at the beginning of the verse to assure you that He is not lying to you? ____________ __________________

Are you going to come into eternal judgment? ❒ YES ❒ NO

Have you passed from spiritual death into life? ❒ YES ❒ NO

Friend, you've just been born again. You just became a child of God.

To help you grow in your new Christian life, we would like to send you some Bible study materials. To receive these helpful materials free of charge, e-mail your request to **info@LamplightersUSA.org.**

Appendix

Level 1 (Basic Training) Student Workbook

To begin, familiarize yourself with the Lamplighters' *Leadership Training and Development Process* (see graphic on page 120). Notice there are two circles: a smaller, inner circle and a larger, outer circle. The inner circle shows the sequence of weekly meetings beginning with an Open House, followed by an 8–14 week study, and concluding with a clear presentation of the gospel (Final Exam). The outer circle shows the sequence of the Intentional Discipleship training process (Leading Studies, Training Leaders, Multiplying Groups). As participants are transformed by God's Word, they're invited into a discipleship training process that equips them in every aspect of the intentional disciple-making ministry.

The Level 1 training (Basic Training) is *free*, and the training focuses on two key aspects of the training: 1) how to prepare a life-changing Bible study (ST-A-R-T) and 2) how to lead a life-changing Bible study (10 commandments). The training takes approximately 60 minutes to complete, and you complete it as an individual or collectively as a small group (preferred method) by inserting an extra week between the Final Exam and the Open House.

To begin your training, go to www.LamplightersUSA.org to register yourself or your group. A Lamplighters' Certified Trainer will guide you through the entire Level 1 training process. After you have completed the training, you can review as many times as you like.

When you have completed the Level 1 training, please consider completing the Level 2 (Advanced) training. Level 2 training will equip you to reach more people for Christ by learning how to train new leaders and by showing you how to multiply groups. You can register for additional training at www.LamplightersUSA.org.

Intentional Discipleship

Training & Development Process

Multiplying Groups

The 5 Steps of Faith for Starting Studies

Training Library

Online Resources

Leading Studies

ST-A-R-T

10 Commandments

Solving All Group Problems

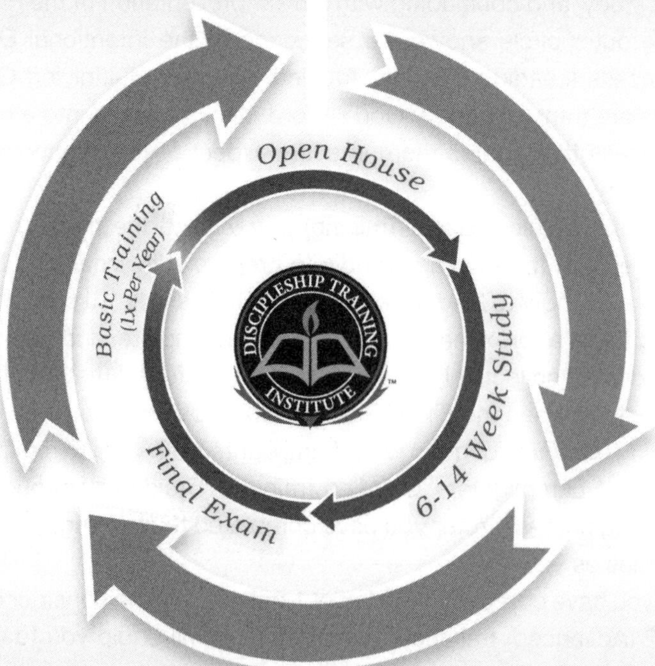

Training Leaders

4 Responsibilities of a Trainer

Leadership Training

4 Levels of Student Development

3 Diagnostic Questions

How to Prepare a Life-Changing Bible Study

ST-A-R-T

Step 1: ______________________ and ______________________.

Pray specifically for the group members and yourself as you study God's Word. Ask God (__________________) to give each group member a rich time of personal Bible study, and thank (_____________) God for giving you a desire to invest in the spiritual advancement of each other.

Step 2: _______________ the ______________________.

Answer the questions in the weekly lessons without looking at the _______________ ___________.

Step 3: _______________ and ______________________.

Review the Leader's Guide, and ________ every truth you missed when you originally did your lesson. Record the answers you missed with a _________ _____________ so you'll know what you missed.

Step 4: _______________ _______________.

Calculate the specific amount of time _______ __________ to spend on each question and write the start time next to each one in the _____________ using a ______________________.

How to Lead a Life-Changing Bible Study

10 COMMANDMENTS

1	2	3
4	5	6
7	8	9
	10	

Lamplighters' 10 Commandments are proven small group leadership principles that have been used successfully to train hundreds of believers to lead life-changing, intentional discipleship Bible studies.

Essential Principles for Leading Intentional Discipleship Bible Studies

1. The 1st Commandment: The ________________ Rule.
   The Leader-Trainer should be in the room ____ minutes before the class begins.

2. The 2nd Commandment: The ________-_____ Rule.
   Train the group that it is okay to ___________, but they should never be ________________.

3. The 3rd Commandment: The __________________ Rule.
   ______________, ______________, ______________ ask for ____________ to ______ the ________, ______, and __________ the questions. The Leader-Trainer, however, should always ______ the questions to control the _______ of the study.

4. The 4th Commandment: The ____:____ Rule.
   _______ the Bible study on time and _____________ the study on time ____________ ________________. No exceptions!

5. The 5th Commandment: The ___________ Rule.
   Train the group participants to ______________ on God's Word for answers to life's questions.

1	2	3
4 59:59	5	6
7	8	9
	10	

6. The 6th Commandment: The ________________ Rule.
   Deliberately and progressively ___________ _____ participants into the group discussion over a period of time.

7. The 7th Commandment: The _________ __________ Rule.
   ___________ the participants to get ________ the answers to the questions, not just _________ or __________ ones.

8. The 8th Commandment: The ____________________ Rule.
   _______________ the group discussion so you _________ the lesson _____ ________ and give each question ________________ ___________.

9. The 9th Commandment: The _____-_________________ Rule.
   Don't let the group members talk about ______________ _______________, _____________ _____________________, or ____________________ _______________.

10. The 10th Commandment: The _____________________ Rule.
    ____________ God to change lives, including ____________.

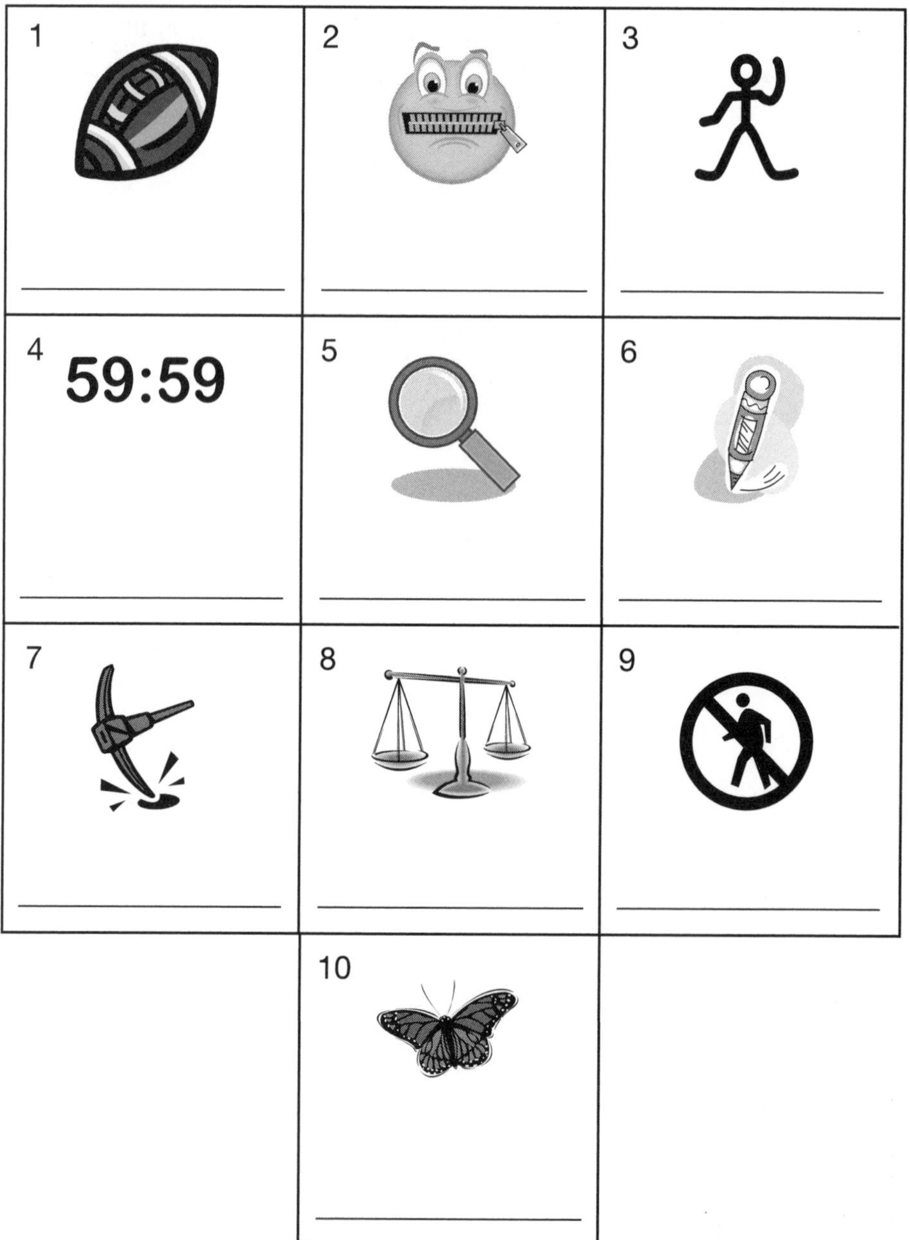
1
2
3
4
59:59
5
6
7
8
9
10

Choose your next study from any of the following titles

- John 1-11
- John 12-21
- Acts 1-12
- Acts 13-28
- Romans 1-8
- Romans 9-16
- Galatians
- Ephesians
- Philippians
- Colossians
- 1 & 2 Thessalonians
- 1 Timothy
- 2 Timothy
- Titus/Philemon
- Hebrews
- James
- 1 Peter
- 2 Peter/Jude

Additional Bible studies and sample lessons are available online.

For audio introductions on all Bible studies, visit us online at www.Lamplightersusa.org.

Looking to begin a new group?
The Lamplighters Starter Kit includes:

- 8 James Bible Study Guides
  (students purchase their own books)
- 25 Welcome Booklets
- 25 Table Tents
- 25 Bible Book Locator Bookmarks
- 50 Final Exam Tracts
- 50 Invitation Cards

For a current listing of live and online discipleship training events, or to register for discipleship training, go to www.LamplightersUSA.org/training.